The *Son*day School Book

Ideas and Techniques for Teaching the Faith

Jeffrey E. Burkart

CPH™
SAINT LOUIS

To
Irwin, Florence,
Mildred, Heinrich,
Martha, Jonathan, David, and Andrew,
and to
all teachers of the faith everywhere

Scripture quotations marked KJV are from the King James or Authorized Version of the Bible.

Scripture quotations marked RSV are from the Revised Standard Version of the Bible, copyrighted 1946, 1952, © 1971, 1973 by the Division of Christian Education of the National Council of the Churches of Christ in the U.S.A., and are used by permission.

Unless otherwise noted, Scripture quotations are taken from THE HOLY BIBLE, NEW INTERNATIONAL VERSION Copyright © 1973, 1978, 1984 by the International Bible Society. Used by permission of Zondervan Publishing House. All rights reserved.

The "NIV" and "New International Version" trademarks are registered in the United States Patent and Trademark Office by the International Bible Society. Use of either trademark requires the permission of the International Bible Society.

Copyright © 1995 Concordia Publishing House
3558 S. Jefferson Avenue, St. Louis, MO 63118-3968
Manufactured in the United States of America

The _Son_day School Book

Ideas and Techniques for Teaching the Christian Faith

Copyright © 1993 by Jeffrey E. Burkart
All rights reserved. No part of this publication may be reproduced, stored in a retrieval system, or transmitted, in any form or by any means, electronic, mechanical, photocopying, recording, or otherwise, without the prior written permission of Concordia Publishing House.

Library of Congress Cataloging-in-Publication Data.

Burkart, Jeffrey E., 1948–
    The sonday [sic] school book : ideas and techniques for teaching the faith/ Jeffrey E. Burkart.
          p.   cm.
     ISBN 0-570-04694-7
     1. Volunteer workers in Christian education. 2. Christian education— Teacher training. I. Title. II. Title: Sunday school book.
    BV1471.2.B79 1995
    268`.6—dc20   94-36253

1 2 3 4 5 6 7 8 9 10   04 03 02 01 00 99 98 97 96 95

Contents

Introduction

FEEDING AND BEING FED: TEACHING THE FAITH TO GOD'S CHILDREN

Over the past 25 years it has been my privilege to speak to thousands of teachers of the faith. During this time I have met with Sunday school teachers, Christian day school teachers, pastors, and directors of Christian education who have encouraged me to put in writing the ideas and techniques for teaching the faith that I have presented in workshop formats.

As you read this book, think about how you go about the task of teaching the Christian faith in both formal and informal settings. Think about how you teach and why you teach. Reflect on what faith is and how we Christians transmit it as we live our lives in faithfulness to our Lord and Savior.

Getting Ready to Feed and Be Fed

Let's feed the lambs by teaching them about the great and wonderful acts of God. Let's feed them so that they grow in their faith. Let's feed them so *they* can tell the story of how God sent his Son into this sinful world to be born, live, die and rise for us.

And in the feeding, remember that you too will be fed. Each time you prepare to teach and tell the story of salvation to children, you teach and tell the story to yourself. Each time you prepare to speak the good news to others, you speak it to yourself.

As we prepare to feed the lambs, we ourselves are being fed on the good news of the Gospel. This is a great arrangement! It's another one of God's surprises. God always gives us more than we ask for—in fact more than we would ever hope to ask for (see Eph. 3:20). Let's be prepared to learn as well as to teach as we go about planning our lessons.

You Are Part of God's Plan

As a teacher, you are a very important part of God's plan for proclaiming the good news of salvation. The time you spend teaching children the faith will have a significant influence on their lives. This can't be said enough. Whenever you teach, you are placed in a situation where the Holy Spirit can work through you to make changes happen in the lives of your students.

Sometimes you will know if an important change in a student's life has occurred. More often, you will not know how their lives have changed. Always remember that the Holy Spirit is working through you to accomplish God's good purposes. As you teach, you will have the opportunity to model your faith-life for your students and help them to understand what it means to be redeemed sons and daughters of God. You can rest assured that your faith-filled teaching and living will have significant impact on the lives of your students.

Working Creatively

Whenever you say the word *creativity* or *creative*, people start to get nervous. Their first reaction is one of denial. "I'm not very creative," they say. However, I have found that people are very creative. Sometimes they need some encouragement, but for the most part, teachers are a most creative group. They will come up with the most unusual, unexpected, unique, and interesting ways of teaching when they are called upon to do so.

Here's the dilemma: When following a lesson in the teacher's guide, teachers may become too dependent on the guide itself and not think of their own creative ways to teach the lesson. A teachers guide can only get you so far; your own personality, enthusiasm, experience, and creativity must take up where the guide leaves off.

I once observed a teacher teaching a lesson with the teachers guide. He held it tightly and hardly looked up from it during the introduction to the lesson. He read the guide *verbatim* and seemed to be totally dependent on it. When it came time to start the main body of the lesson, he read these words: "Read the following passage to the children." Then he caught himself—ooops! This teacher was so bound to the guide that he was reading the directions found on the page margins. If you find yourself doing that, it's time to put the teachers guide away and concentrate on studying the Bible story itself in greater detail.

Creativity is based on rumination, study, patience, cooperation, a sense of humor, careful thought, hard work, and flashes of insight. When hard work, thought, and concentrated study come together, the creative moment has the opportunity to burst into being.

Solving Problems

Teaching creatively presents lots of problems to solve. But problems should not be looked upon in negative ways. We need to think differently about the nature of problem solving.

Every problem presents us with a challenge and an opportunity to learn something new. Every problem holds the possibility for service, learning, creativity, and growth in faith. In our life, God presents us with a series of problems to solve. God also promises to be with us as we solve them and provide the strength to see them through.

I hope that every idea, technique, project, and resource presented in this book poses a problem for you. Maybe the problem will be how to incorporate an idea into your lesson. Perhaps the problem will be that you will find an idea intriguing, but don't feel comfortable implementing it. For veteran teachers, the problem might be that you'll want to throw out something you have always liked to do and replace it with something that is unfamiliar and untried (that's called risk taking and is always a little scary). For new teachers the problem could be trying anything for the first time (that's called risk taking).

Whether you are an experienced teacher or a neophyte, I want you to know that God is going to use your gift of teaching to strengthen the faith of your students. I want you to know that you will have a great impact on the lives of the children whom you teach. Teachers sometimes never find out how much influence they have had on the lives of their students, but I want to assure you that your teaching will be blessed by God and that the children you teach will be blessed also.

How to Begin

Let's begin as we should begin every endeavor: In the name of the Father and the Son and the Holy Spirit. Amen.

Take time to pray right now. Maybe you will pray for guidance and understanding as you read this book. Perhaps you will pray that God will help you be a better teacher. You might ask God's help as you prepare for your Sunday school lessons—or maybe you need to pray something else that is pressing on your heart at this moment that has nothing to do with teaching, but is very important. Whatever it is, now is the time to pray.

Amen! Yes, we agree most heartily! Verily, truly, for sure, for certain! When we teach the faith, we need to start with strong "Amen" language. We need to proclaim the good news to our children so that they can say amen with conviction. We shout not for shouting's sake, but to speak and sing and proclaim it with the strength and assurance of voice which would make a stranger stand and take notice.

That's how we need to teach: with a voice filled with the Gospel message's assurance—with an "Amen" voice. We need to model the Gospel message, to model "at all times and in all places" the life of faith that started in us in our Baptism. Speaking the Gospel with an "Amen voice" and modeling an "Amen life" of faith are important ways to teach children the faith.

Ready to Begin

Now we're really ready to begin. We're ready because God has promised to bless our teaching and to help us as we "feed the lambs." So, let's get started with the first chapter. It deals with six common phrases which are problematic. They are phrases to which we need to respond in positive, creative, problem-solving ways. They are called ... *

* This is what we call a "cliff hanger." It is meant to get you to turn the page right away to find out the next part of the story. It also assumes that you are already guessing what the answer will be. Both children and adults like a surprise, a cliff hanger, or a puzzle.

Think about using cliff hangers in your teaching. Give your students a joyous surprise every day as you help them discover the essential ingredients of faith, forgiveness, and service to others. Are you ready to find out what's next? Well, go ahead. Before you die of curiosity, turn the page and ...

ONE

The Killer Phrases

Killer phrases are statements designed to stop creativity in its tracks. They immediately stifle any and all imaginative thoughts, discussions of new ideas, or actions that might bring about positive change. Killer phrases are common expressions that seem on the surface to be harmless. In reality, they can kill an idea or activity that is worthy of exploration. They are spoken almost without thinking by people who are well-meaning, but hooked on the "killer phrase habit." Be on the lookout for these phrases and learn how to defend against them in positive ways. See if you recognize these phrases and think carefully about any which you may have said yourself.

Killer Phrase 1: "We've Never Done It That Way Before!"

I bet almost everyone who reads this book has either heard this said at a meeting or said it themselves. It is the most common of the killer phrases and one of the most deadly. Sometimes sarcastically referred to as the "seven last words of the church," this killer phrase is so negative that few people can withstand its power. Trying out a new idea or implementing a new program is always a little frightening because most of us like to stick with the "old way of doing things." And, after all ...

Killer Phrase 2: "If It Ain't Broke, Don't Fix It!"

Killer phrases 1 and 2 are meant to keep us from looking at a new idea or trying a different approach. They are especially dangerous for those of us who are trying to seek new ways to teach the great stories of the Bible so that the message of the Gospel will be understood by today's students. If we stick with the old only because it means that we get out of doing a little homework, we are missing a great opportunity to help students grow in their faith and for us to grow in our own faith as well.

My grandma always used the German expression: "Wir bleiben beim Alten!" That's another way of saying, "If it ain't broke, don't fix it!" In German it literally means, "We stick with the old." But even if something isn't broken, it can always be polished, tightened, decorated, welded, added to, enhanced, oiled, strengthened, and reinforced. For example:

My Rusty Oldsmobile

I drive a 1978 Oldsmobile. Since I live in Minnesota, where roads are liberally salted in the winter, my car is suffering from a bad case of rust. My car has 175,215 miles on it now and needs tender, loving care. I would hate to get rid of my car. I want to keep it as long as I can because it's familiar to me. I keep it well oiled and greased so that it will keep on going that extra mile. Each spring I spray on paint and try to put a stop to the rust. I get out my tub of car wax and polish every spot. Last year I bought a buffing wheel that I attach to my power drill and whirrrrrr away at what's left of my car's finish until it looks showroom new (well close to it anyway). I take a bottle of spray stuff and go over the dash board and every plastic part of my old Olds until the interior is shining with a kind of greasy gloss. I do the same thing to my tires. Even though they have no tread left, it makes me feel safer if the sidewalls look new.

Now, here's the point! If you want to stick with the old, you'll still have to keep working on it if you want to keep it fresh. Even if you have taught the story of Jonah 20 times, you have to keep polishing it. The old stories need to be freshened up through elbow grease—that is, study, reflection, prayer, and preparation. If we work on polishing the way we teach the stories of the Bible, they will take on a new appearance. They'll still be the "old story," but they will look new to you and sound new to your students. Eventually my old Olds will end up in a scrap heap. Bible stories, on the other hand, only get better with use—they have an unlimited mileage guarantee.

Don't let killer phrases 1 and 2 stop you from trying out something new or polishing up your tried and true lessons. If you have experimented with a new idea or discovered a special way of teaching a lesson, share it with your brother and sister teachers.

A Word About Sharing (Well, actually, several words)

Sharing your plans with others is a great way to try out your lessons. Before I teach a lesson, give a chapel talk, or make a presentation, I always try to tell someone about it. Sometimes I try my ideas, songs, or stories out on my own children (my toughest critics). If they respond favorably, I know I'm on the right track. I know that sharing can sometimes be a little worrisome. It means taking the risk that someone may tell you they don't like your idea. More likely than not, your idea will be liked.

The important thing is for you to tell someone about it. Sharing with others provides you the opportunity to practice your lesson and to receive some suggestions on how it might be improved. Practicing your lessons on others (especially your friends) is a great way of engaging them in Christian conversation. Whenever Christians start talking together about their faith and how to better share that faith with children, the Spirit of God is there to make good things happen. Sharing, in and of itself, is a good exercise. It helps us clarify our goals and strengthens our ability to communicate the meaning of the stories we teach.

Killer Phrase 3: "Let's Form a Committee!"

Committees can be very useful. When large amounts of work need to be done or when approval from a variety of people is necessary, a committee is essential. Not every task needs a committee to do the work. Sometimes it is more effective to do it yourself or to get one person to help you rather than to wait for a committee to meet. Remember that it is the individual teacher who really makes things happen. Your energy, enthusiasm, and skill is what will make an idea fly. Don't allow an idea or project to go by the wayside because a committee is unable to meet or slow to get started. Use committees wisely lest they become a hindrance rather than an effective means toward positive change. If your project or idea must come before a committee, however, you must beware of the next killer phrase.

Killer Phrase 4: "Let's Table It!"

This favorite phrase kills an idea through the use of parliamentary procedure. It is commonly used in committee meetings, although it is not limited to them. If an idea or project is tabled it may die a long and painful death. Letting something die on the table is just as bad as letting it die in committee—the results are the same.

Before you present an idea to a committee, make sure that you have done lots of thinking about it. Try to present your ideas as completely as you can. Talk to as many people as you can about your idea before you present it. Get feedback from key people (especially committee members) so that you can articulate your ideas clearly. Take their advice seriously and don't get upset if they are not as excited about your idea as you are. If your idea has merit, people will want to support it. A well-presented, thoroughly-prepared idea that has been discussed with committee members before it comes to the floor will have a much better chance to succeed.

Here are some ideas that you might wish to try out. See if you can identify ones that need some kind of committee approval and those that you can do yourself or with the help of one friend.

1. Adopting a new Sunday school curriculum series

2. Doing a puppet show based on the Gospel lessons of the day to be performed in church

3. Making a video of your class's visit to a nursing home

4. Starting a Sunday school newsletter

5. Doing a musical based on the story of Noah and the ark*

6. Redoing a lesson plan on David and Goliath

7. Having your eighth-grade class sing some songs for the kindergartners

8. Making individual chalkboards for your class (I'll tell you how to make them in *The Sonday School Book II.*)

9. Starting a family choir that will sing in church during the summer "off choir" months (rehearsals to be held during the last 15 minutes of Bible class hour)

10. Purchasing a children's hymnal or other kind of song book for use in Sunday school or Christian day school*

11. Sending out baptismal birthday cards to your students*

12. Asking each of your students to bring some old magazines to class

13. Buying an electric synthesizer for use with the children's choir

14. Attending a workshop sponsored by a local church

15. Developing a food shelf for the hungry or having students do volunteer service at a food shelf as part of a service project to be sponsored by your church

16. Having your students visit a shut-in or someone in the hospital

17. Having your students write a get-well card to someone in their class that is ill

18. Making a personal visit to each parent of the students whom you teach (especially Sunday school parents)

19. Organizing a field trip to another church in your neighborhood

20. Taking a group of young people to a local or national youth gathering

* See the Resource List, page 148.

You can see that some things can be done independently, while others will probably need some kind of approval. In any case, try to share your ideas with others to receive feedback regarding your plans. Again, by telling others about your ideas, you will help to clarify your own goals and become better able to explain exactly what you would like to do.

Let's pretend that you have just come up with an idea that will need some approval. You start to share you idea with someone and they hit you with the following killer phrase:

Killer Phrase 5: "That's a Good Idea, But It's Not the Right Time for It."

This killer phrase is a variant of "Let's table it." When is the right time to do something? Anytime that you want to try out a new idea (especially if it involves lots of people) you will probably hear Killer Phrase 5. This one is tough to counter. Everyone is pressed for time today. Because people are usually jealous of their time, they automatically react negatively to any kind of imposition on it. When you ask for someone's time, you are really asking for something important. Time is life. Whenever we decide to do a task, we are really deciding how much of our life's time we are willing to spend to accomplish it. Our time, like our life, is a precious gift from God and we should try to do everything we can to use it wisely.

Put It on the Calendar!

If someone says "it's not the right time," counter with a proposal "to put it on the calendar." You might agree that you can't accomplish the task this week. But what about a month from now? Or next year? It may be legitimate to say that the time isn't right, but that shouldn't stop you from doing it at the right time.

Many good lesson ideas, service projects, worship opportunities, and other worthy activities die at the hands of Killer Phrase 5 simply because they never get past the killer phrase and put it down in writing on the calendar. The calendar is one of the most important tools to help you accomplish any task.

Once an idea is placed on the calendar, it will take on a life of its own. A project on the calendar has a very good chance of actually happening. If it's on the calendar, it means that it is a priority item. This is true for big events (choir concerts, festival or Holy Day worship services) and for day-to-day lesson preparation (making a puppet or flannelgraph to tell a Bible story, ordering a movie) as well. More on this when we talk about lesson preparation in another chapter. For now, remember that it is essential to schedule your ideas on a calendar so that your ideas have a chance to come alive.

Killer Phrase 6: "We Don't Have It in the Budget!"

There it is! The Mt. Everest of Killer Phrases. All others pale in comparison. Like time, money is not unlimited. But don't be discouraged by that. For over 25 years I have taught in and worked with schools that have limited financial resources. My experience has shown me that there are creative ways to get around the money issue. Yes, they are legal. Just because they're creative doesn't mean that they're naughty.

Let me give you an example. One of my former students had an idea. She wanted to take 35mm color slides of her children's Christmas art projects and project them on a screen during her church's Christmas Eve service. She didn't have a camera, film, close-up lens (or a macro lens), nor did her church own a 35mm slide projector. The church had a projection screen, but it was broken. (This is what is referred to by presidents, generals, and think-tank people as a worst-case scenario.)

Here is the cost breakdown in "killer phrase—worst-case scenario" terminology:

1. One 35mm single lens reflex camera (cheapest available from discount store) = $175.00

2. One roll of slide film = $6.50

3. One set of close-up lenses = $25.00, or one macro lens = $235.00

4. One 35mm slide projector = $450.00

5. One projection screen = $200.00

6. One roll of slide film developed = $6.50

Total Cost: Somewhere between $863.00 and $1,073.00. Result: Idea is kaput!

Here is the cost if we used a positive creative approach.
1. One 35mm single-lens, reflex camera (borrowed from a member of the congregation who is a photography person.) This person probably has a darkroom and all the photographic equipment needed to do this simple job. Cost: $0.00

2. One roll of 35mm color slide film, if donated, costs $0.00. If not donated, go to the cheapest discount store near you. Cost: $5.50–$6.50.

3. A set of close-up lenses or a macro lens borrowed from a friendly photographer. Cost: $0.00

4. One 35mm slide projector borrowed from members of the church who

bought one for the purpose of showing slides of their Hawaiian vacation in 1983. They have not used the slide projector since then. It is collecting dust in their basement, and they are probably willing to lend it to you on a permanent basis. Send out a request for a slide projector in your church's newsletter, or have your pastor ask for the loan of a projector at the next adult Bible class hour. Every congregation has someone with an unused projector sitting at home. You may also be able to borrow one from your public library or from the audio/visual specialist at your local public school. (This sometimes goes for video equipment as well.) Cost: $0.00

5. Most churches and schools have a working projection screen. However, you can easily make a projection screen with a white, king-size bed sheet that is stretched across a wooden frame. See the diagram on page 87. Cost: $0.00 to $5.00.

6. One roll of developed slide film. Cost: $6.50.

Approximate cost for this approach: $12.00 to $18.00, compared to $863.00 to $1,073.00.

Result: Go for it! What a deal! (My former student actually did this project for her church's Christmas Eve program for a cost of about $15.00. The borrowed slide projector and homemade screen have found a permanent home in her church.)

A Positive Approach ...

Throughout all this talk about killer phrases, I hope that you have seen an underlying positive approach to solving problems. Killer phrases are couched in language filled with words such as "not," "don't," and "never." As we teach the faith we need to use vocabulary that has a positive ring. Instead of killer phrases, we speak in resurrection phrases, phrases that build up, strengthen, and edify each other. We need to choose and use words that are winsome and filled with confidence, words that can trigger new ideas, actions, and harmony.

With this positive approach in mind, we can turn to a topic that needs to be addressed by every teacher. The topic of ...

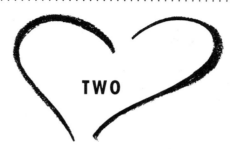

TWO

Discipline: Teaching Disciplined Disciples

Whether you're an experienced professional educator or a first-time Sunday school teacher, you are going to run into some kind of disciplinary problem. Discipline (sometimes called behavioral management) is a complex topic; we can't cover every aspect of it, but we can help to get you started in the right direction.

In this chapter I want to: 1) share some specific, practical ideas that will help you to focus basic ways to halt discipline problems before they begin; 2) give some generic advice regarding general approaches to discipline; and 3) discuss how *Christian* teachers discipline.

But first, a story.

Not too long ago I was speaking to a group of Sunday school teachers. Of all the people there, the one I remember most was a woman who was now several months into her 51st year of dedicated Sunday school teaching. For 50 years she had taught children in the lower grades, but this year was different; she had volunteered to teach the junior high school kids. The Sunday school superintendent had asked for a volunteer to teach the junior high class (13 children in 7th and 8th grade in this case), but there were no takers. She took the job.

Junior-high-school-age students present unique challenges to parents and teachers alike. This brave woman of experience volunteered because she thought she would enjoy the challenge. She was in for a surprise.

As we talked at the lunch table, she looked over at me and said, "You know, those kids act like jerks!" Silence swept over the table. I'm sure that the people at the table were not used to hearing this saintly lady speak in such graphic terms. She looked around at the stunned faces and said with all boldness, "Well, they are!"

I was always taught to respect my elders, so it's a little hard for me to correct, let alone chastise someone who is older than I am (especially someone who is old enough to be my grandma). Therefore, I carefully broached the subject of discipline with her. I reminded her that God wants us to give special attention to the "jerks"; to minister to them the most because they need it the most. It must have been the way that I said it, because everyone laughed (including the lady in question) and the tension was eased.

Then I said, "Now tell me really, are all of them jerks or just some of them?" She laughed again and said, "Well, just a few, I guess."

"How many are really giving you a problem?" I asked.

"Well, there's this one boy … " Then she went on to explain how this one student was making her life difficult.

This lady was making a common mistake; she allowed one person's behavior to influence her perception of the behavior of all the students. Only one junior high schooler was causing trouble, but her feelings about the entire class were altered because of one child's behavior. This attitude made it difficult for her to face the children on Sunday because she felt that she was going to fight a battle that she could not win. She went on to explain that she had taught most of these children when they were in her second grade class and that she was not prepared for the changes that had taken place in them since that time. She felt that she was out of touch with them.

I'm sure that many of us empathize with this teacher regardless of which grade level we teach or how long we have taught. A behavioral problem can make everything seem to go wrong and sour our teaching day. So how can we avoid the discipline problems? Well, we can't. No matter how hard we try there will always be some kind of discipline problem to solve. But we can try to stack the deck in our favor if we are proactive in our approach to discipline.

It is not possible to give you an answer to every behavior problem that you'll have during the next year. It is possible to suggest some strategies that will help ward off discipline problems and minimize them. Remember, there is no absolutely sure set of actions that will insure the elimination of behavioral problems. If anyone tries to tell you there is, they are probably selling you a snake-oil remedy. No quick fixes or snake-oil remedies here—just some ways that I have found helpful in curbing problems before they start.

Visiting Children in Their Homes with Their Parents before School Starts

There is probably no better way to start the school year (Sunday school or weekday school) than to take the time to do a home visit. Your first reaction may be, "How will I get the time to do this? I've got 16 kids in my Sunday school class. I'll never be able to see everyone before school starts. [Etc.]"

There is no doubt that a home visit takes time. However, it is time well spent because it accomplishes a number of important things:

1. **It allows you to *establish a relationship* with the child in the child's own environment.**

Because the classroom is your turf, it may not be the best place to build rapport with children (especially children whom you have never met). Getting to know children in their own home is much more comfortable for them. It also affords you the opportunity to meet with their parents.

2. **It helps you to establish a relationship with parents.**

Meeting the parents or guardians of the children you teach is as important as meeting the child. It is essential because the child's Christian education greatly needs the support of the family. By getting to know the family you will gain insights into the nature of the child. You will find out about the concerns that parents have and may even find out about some behavior patterns (for good or ill) that their child has demonstrated in the past.

Meeting the parents is an excellent way of showing your concern for their child's spiritual growth. It will help parents to see that you are in a partnership with them that is designed to foster their child's spiritual well-being. Parents will appreciate your visit and will be more supportive of you because of the time you have taken to get to know them and their child.

3. It gives you insight into the spiritual life of the family.

Meeting with parents can also be important because you can't assume that all parents understand the message of the Gospel.

Whenever I speak to a group of Christian teachers, I ask this question: "How many of your student's parents know that *they* are redeemed by God in Christ Jesus?" Without exception I have found that every Christian church, school, Sunday school, and vacation Bible school has children in attendance whose parents have not heard the Good News.

The home visit gives you an opportunity to explain the Gospel message to parents who may not know Christ, even though they send their children to Christian-education instruction. Never assume that all parents are Christian just because they send their children to your school. There are many social, emotional, and quasi-spiritual reasons that influence parents and guardians to send their children to church for biblical instruction. Establishing a relationship with parents will enable you to do a better job of proclaiming the Gospel not only to the child, but to the parents as well.

Meeting with the family (you might even meet a grandparent or two) will give the family time to ask you some questions about the expectations you have regarding behavior. This gives you the chance to explain how your class will be structured. This is especially important for children who are new to your school and for younger children who may feel a bit strange about going to their first Sunday school class.

4. Establishing a positive, working relationship with the parents will help if a discipline problem does arise.

If it ever becomes necessary to report a problem to the parents, it is important to have established a relationship so that you can share a frank, positive discussion of the problem.

I once had a parent tell me the following: "If my kid gives you any trouble, give him a good whack and let me know so that I can give him one when he gets home." This gave me a good indication of what kind of discipline was used at home and made me very sensitive to the needs of that child. I was thankful that I didn't have any problems that needed reporting, because I'm sure that this parent would have overreacted to almost anything. It's important to know the parents for any number of reasons.

What to Do for a Home Visit

1. Send a post card to parents informing them you will be calling to set up a time to meet with them and their child. If you have a newsletter that reaches every parent, use it to announce that home visits will be sched-

uled in the near future. If parents know you will be calling for an appointment, it does not come as a surprise and will help them anticipate your call and respond favorably to it.

2. Call parents on the phone and set up an appointment to meet with them and their child. The meeting does not have to be long (15 minutes may be plenty of time to do the job).

3. Take some sample lessons along when you meet with the family to show them what you will be doing during the first few weeks. You might also prepare a calendar of upcoming worship activities in which their child will be participating. Parents appreciate knowing when the Sunday school Christmas program will be and which Sundays their children will be singing in church. This gives parents a chance to ask questions about what their children will be doing and what expectations you have of their child. In short, "An informed parent is a happy parent."

4. Ask the parents or child to fill out a file card for your reference. The file card could contain the following information:

   a. Name of the child

   b. Name of parents (guardians, Godparents, and grandparents can also be listed)

   c. Address—important to know so that you can send a note to the parents when their child does something noteworthy.

   d. Home and work phone numbers (for reminders about upcoming events or to tell them that their child is doing well in school)

   e. Child's birthday and date of Baptism—important to know so that you can send a birthday and Baptism-birthday card to the child.

   Note: If you find that the child has not been baptized, be careful not to make either the child or the parents feel uncomfortable about it. If people don't understand what Baptism is, you will need to take time to explain its significance. The home visit may or may not be the appropriate place to do so. In any case, you will probably want to inform your pastor, Sunday school superintendent, director of evangelism or Christian outreach, Christian school principal, or other appropriate people so that the family is approached in a winsome, evangelical way. Here you must use your "spiritual savvy" to decide upon the best course of action. Talk about this with your pastor before you go out on your visit. Try to discuss these ideas with your staff before you implement them so that you feel confident and comfortable with the process. We must avoid giving people the impression that they are "second-class spiritual citizens" because they do not understand Baptism.

Have Your Classroom Ready and Meet the Students at the Door

This is good advice for every class period, but it is especially important on the first day of class. The first day you meet with students is probably the most crucial one for establishing the routines and expectations which you have for the class. Being ready means that you have all your materials set to go, desks or chairs in the arrangement that you think will work best, and attendance procedures figured out in advance. As students come in, try to meet them at the door and call them by name. If you don't remember their names, now is the time to memorize. Knowing names is part of good preparation and will help you in classroom management. Take the time to imagine what you would do to prepare the room, the lesson and yourself for the perfect start of the year. Then go about trying to do everything you can to make that perfect start happen.

Discuss Your Behavioral Expectations Right Away

In respect to discipline, discuss the expectations that you *and* the children have for classroom behavior. Appropriate classroom conduct is not generated by merely listing a set of rules. Appropriate classroom behavior is best achieved when students and teachers discuss the reasons for behaving in appropriate, positive ways. By discussing the positive, appropriate behaviors with children you will afford them the opportunity to think about their actions before they act. A discussion centered on establishing high expectations gives the class the chance to think about the consequences of their actions. A listing of teacher-made rules does not allow children to take ownership of the rules.

Express Expectations in Positive Terms

Once a discussion of positive expectations begins, you can start to list them in positive terms. This differs from the way we usually express rules. Here is a short list of common classroom rules expressed in the negative:

1. Don't run in the classroom or in the halls.

2. Don't talk unless you raise your hand.

3. Don't get out of your seat unless you have teacher's permission.

4. Don't butt in line.

5. Don't push each other at the drinking fountain.

While these rules are good rules to follow, they are all going to be broken at one time or another during the course of the day. (Remember the old saying, "Rules are meant to be broken.") Children are notorious at finding ways around the rules and making up excuses to justify their actions when they are caught breaking them.

Begin by discussing the reasons *why* certain actions are appropriate. Then you may stand a better chance of having children think before they act in an inappropriate way. Try starting a discussion of classroom expectations with a question regarding conduct in the classroom. Ask children to tell what they think is important regarding behavior and list kinds of behaviors that are most appropriate in the classroom. For example: "How should we behave in the classroom and in the hallways of our school?" Here the answers will vary, but eventually you will get around to a list of positive behaviors that are generated by the children. A short list of positive behaviors might look like this:

1. Walk in the classroom or halls. Why? Because we are concerned for

safety, because we understand that other people might be disturbed, etc.

2. Be patient as you wait for your turn at the drinking fountain. Why? Because if you push each other, you might cause an accident at the fountain and hurt someone by mistake, etc.

3. Listen carefully to what other people are saying. Why? Because we often learn from hearing other people's ideas and stories, etc.

A discussion of expectations goes beyond the mere listing of rules. It enables children to understand the reasons for acting differently in the class-room than they do on the playground or at home. It allows them to see behaviors that may be acceptable in one place may not always be appropriate in another and to think about the consequences of their actions before they act.

In this way we actually start to *teach* discipline. A set of rules will not necessarily teach. Rules are external devices used to control or curb behavior, but teaching discipline through a discussion of expectations helps students to learn how to control their behavior and to know what is expected of them in various situations. By helping students understand why certain behaviors are appropriate or inappropriate, they become internally disciplined disciples—people who not only agree with the teachings, but also assist in spreading them because of what they believe.

Obeying the letter of the law without understanding its spirit is not really obeying the law. The rule "raise your hand before you ask a question" is no guarantee that the child will not disturb the class with unnecessary waving and grunting to get someone's attention. We have all seen children raise their hands and begin a wide range of exaggerated, theatrical behaviors that are disruptive.

Teach by Practicing Appropriate Behaviors

Spend some time practicing appropriate behaviors with children during the first class period. By practicing appropriate ways to walk, speak, sharpen a pencil, clean up a mess, and raise one's hand, children will both understand and internalize appropriate behaviors.

Demonstrate the best behaviors during the first class period. A little time spent on learning what is expected will save you a lot of time later. Once students have done a little practicing, they will start to understand how to conduct themselves when in your presence and they will understand how to behave when you are not there. A brief story will explain what I mean.

I once taught a class of fourth graders. The school playground where I taught was covered with very small crushed stones and throwing them was against the rules. One day one of my students (We shall call the student Kim—the name has been changed to protect the innocent.) threw a handful of stones at a group of kids for no reason in particular. No one was hurt by the stones, but predictably the children grabbed a handful of stones and threw them back at the offender. I intervened quickly and called all parties aside.

When the teacher tells a group of kids to stop playing, a sort of domino effect takes place on the playground. One by one everyone stops playing and looks right at the teacher to see what he's going to do. It's sort of a playground version of gaper's block. Since everybody in the fourth grade was looking at us anyway, I decided to do a little demonstration teaching.

I called everybody over and explained what had happened. Apologies and promises were exchanged regarding a non-stone-throwing pact. This was not enough as far as I was concerned.

First we talked about why we shouldn't throw stones and what the consequences of throwing stones could be. Everyone agreed that throwing stones was to be avoided. I then asked every child to pick up a handful of stones and stand ready to throw them against the brick wall of the gym. (I did the same.) Then I asked them what they should do if they found themselves holding a handful of stones on the playground. As you might imagine, they said that they should throw the stones. After a few laughs we agreed that the appropriate response should be to drop the stones. So we all let the stones trickle through our fingers to the ground. After recess we talked about the incident again and I tried to expand on some ideas of how we could avoid problems on the playground.

About a week later some children were taunting Kim on the playground. I was leaning out of sight against the gym wall, but I was able to see and hear everything that transpired. Kim had heard one too many nasty comments so he reached down and grabbed a handful of stones. I was about to yell out when a strange thing happened. Kim shook the stones a couple of times and then let them fall from his fingers. You could almost see the wheels of his mind grinding away as he remembered to think before he acted. I ran right over to him and told him that I was proud that he had remembered to drop the stones. He smiled and told me that he was glad too. I then proceeded to discuss the problem of name calling with certain other fourth graders, but that's another story. It seems that the task of teaching discipline is a never ending one.

The End.

Moral: Demonstrating appropriate behaviors to students and giving them a chance to practice those behaviors will help students to think about their actions and apply what they have learned when similar situations arise.

Here's a list of common classroom behaviors to practice with your students. Use your judgment regarding the appropriateness for different grade levels. You may think of behaviors to practice with your students.

1. Raising hands to speak. (Note: You may wish to tell students that they don't have to keep their hands in the air while others are speaking. Once you see a hand go up, a nod to the student may be sufficient to tell her that she will be called on next. In upper grades, raising hands may not be necessary if orderly discussion behaviors are taught.)

2. Sharpening pencils

3. Asking to be excused from class

4. Answering questions

5. Disagreeing with someone's point of view

6. Cleaning up after working on a messy project

7. Taking attendance

8. Dismissing class

9. Taking turns

10. Working in small groups

11. Reading aloud

12. Listening attentively

13. Watching a demonstration

14. Washing hands

15. Distributing books and other materials

16. Watching a videotape or filmstrip

17. Actively listening to others

18. Preparing to sing in church

19. Sharing

20. Hanging up coats and hats

21. Putting things back in their proper place

List some of your own routine behavioral concerns here:

_____

_____

_____

_____

_____

Analyze Who Is Giving You the Problem

Every student will at one time or another misbehave. However, it is seldom that all students will misbehave at the same time and with the same degree of, shall we say, enthusiasm. If you analyze behavioral problems, you will more than likely find that only a few individuals are disruptive. Avoid the natural tendency to blame the whole group for the actions of one or two students who cause a problem (remember my story about the grandma who thought junior-high students were "*all* jerks"). Once you have analyzed the problem, you can focus on the causes of disruptive behavior.

Keep in mind, though, that we live our lives as both saints and sinners. We are sinful creatures who have been forgiven by God. Living a life of discipleship is one of constant tension between our sinful nature and our forgiven state of grace. As we discipline our children we should keep in mind this saint/sinner existence.

Because of Jesus' sacrifice on the cross we know that God loves us. We show that love to children and help them understand it a little better every day. We don't help children to understand their relationship with God when we hit them with statements made in the heat of anger. We need not apologize when it is necessary to speak words of law to students. However, we also have an obligation to distinguish when we should speak God's condemning words and when we should speak only for ourselves.

Children certainly need to be taught to recognize when they have broken God's law, but they also must be taught that with repentance there is forgiveness. Harsh, unthinking statements, made in anger may drive children away from you. If this happens, you may find it difficult to win them back.

Choose your discipline words with care so that children will understand why you are upset and what they have done to cause you to be so. Try to speak to them so they know how to tell the difference between when *you* are upset and when *God* is upset. This is especially true for the minor annoyances that happen during the course of the day. Try to send children the right message. Don't carelessly say, "Jesus doesn't like you when you do that." That's not what you really mean. Send the right message: "Joe, I am upset with the way you're acting. Please don't do that." This message will give the child an opportunity to think about his behavior and respond appropriately.

Both children and adults often do things without thinking. If we start teaching discipline by discussing our saint/sinner relationship, we will have a foundation for thinking and reacting to discipline problems when they come up. We will be able to handle minor problems with greater ease and difficult problems with carefully chosen words of condemnation and compassion.

Knowing when to speak words of condemnation and how to speak them is something more akin to an art than a science. Sometime in the future you will probably say a condemning word when you shouldn't. You will make mistakes. When you do, you must ask for forgiveness from the children whom you teach. I have had to do this many times during my teaching career. I'm always amazed at how children can forgive and, in so doing, teach the teacher how much the Gospel means. When we forgive one another, we become closer not only to each other, but to God as well. Because of the relationship that God has established with us through our Baptism, we now can live in a forgiven and forgiving relationship with one another in Christ, our Savior.

When a Behavioral Problem Arises, Deal with It Swiftly

When a behavioral problem arises, try to deal with it right away. This doesn't mean blow up at someone for a minor disturbance. You may wish to talk to the child after class to find out what the problem was. In any case, the longer you wait to solve the problem the more likely it will become more severe.

Whatever you do, never use the following when teaching discipleship:
1. "If you had more faith, you would obey me better."

2. "Jesus doesn't like you when you do that."

3. "You'll never get to heaven if you talk like that."

4. "You must not come from a very Christian home if you act that way."

5. "God will punish you if you keep doing that."

I have heard Christian teachers say these lines to children. Some of them have been said to me. These lines are unacceptable in any circumstance. The damage they can do is considerable. These statements are made out of desperation by people who are frustrated beyond their ability to think clearly. Is the child's eternal salvation really at stake because he/she has misbehaved in your classroom? Sometimes children misbehave out of ignorance or because they want attention. Their misbehavior may be a cry for help.

Therefore, distinguish between actions that are calculated, and actively evil from those that merely fail to live up to expectations. Be sensitive to what lies behind behavior. There is a difference between disturbances and planned, active, creative sinning. It is our job to be good classroom managers and distinguish between the two. By calling down the wrath of God on students, we are using Jesus as the controlling force instead of helping students learn to become self-disciplined children of God. We are abdicating our responsibilities as the leader and teacher and are passing "the disciplinary buck" to God.

Indeed, if children are actively and belligerently sinning, a word of law is certainly in order. The law's condemning power serves, in that case, to drive sinners toward repentance. When repentance is shown, we are to swiftly forgive the penitent; they must be assured that their sin has been forgotten by us and by God.

As we teach discipline to others, we have a responsibility to discipline *ourselves* and to remember that God disciplines those he loves (Heb. 12:5–10). Using statements that club children into submission isn't a good way to make them disciplined disciples. We should always try to help children understand that God is their friend and that through their Baptism they live in a relationship of forgiveness with him. That's where discipleship begins and that's where teaching the faith should always begin.

Children must be taught that though we live under God's forgiveness we have not been given a license to sin. Rather, we must proclaim the message that in our Baptism God has made us his own and that the Holy Spirit is at work in us to help us live our lives in service to God and to those people whom he places in our path. (See Romans 6 for more on this.)

Be Equally as Swift to Give Praise for a Job Well Done

When children are working diligently, paying attention, and actively engaged in the lesson, we should make sure that we tell them how pleased we are with them. Children welcome words of encouragement and thanks. When students do something that is beyond the call of duty or is particularly helpful to you, make sure that you tell them. In addition, you may give the parents a telephone call and commend their child's behavior. This will give you another chance to build positive relationships with parents. All parents like to hear a teacher praise their children. When parents hear praise from you, they will share your words with their children and the positive cycle of praise will continue. Sometimes a thank-you note to children will be a good way of expressing your appreciation. Parents who read the note will also appreciate your thoughtfulness.

It is easy to forget to say thanks for a job well done. Sometimes it seems easier to criticize than to recognize all the good things that happen around us. Try to remind yourself to speak words of praise and thanks to children whenever and wherever you can. When we praise and rejoice in good things children do, we teach them how to praise and rejoice as well. If we don't model praise, how can children be expected to know how and when to rejoice and give praise? Seek out opportunities to thank, praise, and rejoice with children.

Relationship, Relationship, Relationship

I know that I've used the word *relationship* a number of times in this chapter. I have done so on purpose because of its extreme importance in the teaching of discipline. The more you know the children you teach, the better you will be able to help them become disciplined disciples. That's why I have stressed things such as: home visits, learning names, knowing birthday and Baptism day, meeting students at the door.

Remember that every child's world is complex. Children are influenced by many people during their average day. The more of these influences you know about, the better you will be able to relate to the child and to those who have significant impact on the child's life.

Knowing the child and his or her parents, understanding the home situation, discovering something about the child's interests, hobbies, and pets, etc., will help you understand the nature of the child. Understanding the nature of children and developing a loving concern for their specific needs is essential for teaching. All children need to be loved and to show love in return. They all need to feel safe and secure. They need to feel accepted by both their classmates and their teachers. All children need to learn, to know, and to dream. Most important of all, children need to know that God loves them so much that he sent his only Son, Jesus, to be their savior.

By building strong relationships with children and their families you will better understand how to meet the needs of the children whom God has entrusted to your care, to discipline them in love, and to joyfully proclaim forgiveness.

Take the Time to Pray about Your Teaching

In working through the challenge of teaching disciplined disciples, we need to take time to talk to God about our concerns.

A Teacher's Prayer

Most gracious Lord Jesus, you are the greatest teacher.
Help me to teach my children as you taught your disciples.
Give me a clear mind and a loving spirit as I go about my teaching today.
Help me to discipline them in love as you disciplined your disciples.
Be my guide as I try to model your teaching as I teach.
Grant me understanding when I feel unsure.
Give me patience when I feel pressed.
Send your Spirit to guide my words and actions that I might teach in ways

that will proclaim your saving grace in Christ Jesus.

All these things I ask in the name of God the Father, my creator and sustainer; God the Son, my redeemer; and God the Holy Spirit, my comforter and friend. Amen.

The Job Is Never Done

As I said at the beginning of this chapter, there is no sure-fire, perfectly correct set of ways to teach discipline. We may go about this task with a great deal of fear and trembling, but go about it we must. I hope that these suggestions will help you to think about how *you* will go about teaching disciplined discipleship. I hope that you will think about and discuss these suggestions with your brother and sister teachers of the faith. I pray that you are blessed as you teach and that your children will be blessed as well.

Another Ingredient

Helping students to become disciplined disciples is important because teaching can't be done effectively where discipline is absent. Our English words *discipline* and *disciple* both come from the same Latin root words: *discipulus* (pupil) and *discere* (to learn). Pupils will learn best in a disciplined environment, but there is another essential ingredient which is needed for effective teaching and learning. This essential ingredient is …

Preparation ... Preparation ... Preparation ...

There is no substitute for it, there is no way around it, and you will be in a heap of trouble if you don't take the time to do it. Preparation, like discipline, is an essential ingredient for teaching. In this chapter I would like to focus on ways that you prepare to prepare for teaching. I'm not talking about writing the lesson plan itself, as important as that is. Teachers guides usually have ample suggestions on how to structure the lesson. The problems I'd like to address come from lack of preparation for teaching on the part of the teacher. Reliance on the teachers guide can lead to a false sense of security. You may believe that since someone else has already done the preparation, all you need to do is follow the cookbook recipe for the perfect lesson every time.

Any of you who have ever tried to teach by merely following the cookbook know that doesn't always work very well. If you only try to imitate a lesson that someone else has written, without taking the time to internalize it and make it your own, you will only be mouthing someone else's words. You may get through the material, but you will not have really taught the children.

Teaching Children, Not Material

It can't be stressed enough! Whenever you are teaching, you are not merely teaching the material, you are teaching *children*. Before we start preparing, our first question should not be *what* are we teaching this week, but *who* are we teaching. Teaching begins when we start to address the needs and nature of the children. We choose the materials and the subject matter that we teach on the basis of how they will best meet the needs of the children. Once we have identified those needs, we can proceed to write objectives and organize the content of our individual lessons.

The vast majority of curriculum materials that we purchase have been written by Christian educators who are highly experienced and skilled teachers of the faith. They have taken great care to develop curricula to help you present a coherent series of lessons built on the great themes of the Scriptures. They have organized the content of the lessons to meet the general spiritual needs of children and have carefully included the topics of sin, forgiveness, God's covenant relationship, Christ's atonement, worship, the resurrection, and other great truths of the Scriptures. There is, however, a problem that still needs to be addressed: These materials must be taught to children *by you*. You will be the one who will teach to the specific needs of the children.

Making the Lesson Your Own

When you teach a lesson, it must become your lesson, your personal property. You are the one who must buy into the materials, methods, and sequence of lessons. You must figure out when to stick with the plan and when to deviate from it. Just because you have purchased a set of curriculum material doesn't mean that you have to follow it to the letter. You will need to make judgments regarding how to teach each lesson and how to accomplish its goals. You will do this because you are a unique individual with thoughts, dreams, and ideas of your own. Making the lesson your own means that you will go beyond the teachers guide and expand on the ideas it presents. The teachers guide is a great starting place. It will contain excellent ideas and well-structured lessons, but it must still be studied, reflected on, and modified to fit your teaching style and the particular needs of your children.

Lessons Are Never Taught in a Vacuum

Whenever possible, teachers should try to relate the Bible stories and lessons to what is currently happening in the world of the child. Between the writing and the publication of any set of lessons there is always a time gap. Several months or even years come between the writing, publication, and the actual teaching of a lesson. There is no way for the writer of the lesson to account for the intervening historical events that will have an influence on the lessons that you teach. If a major event takes place during the week (an outbreak of war in Turkey, an earthquake in Peru, a presidential election), you need to be ready to incorporate something about it in your lesson.

I vividly remember how my youngest son, Andrew, was transfixed by the sight of bombs dropping on Iraq during the Desert Storm military campaign. When I asked him what he was thinking, he simply replied, "Scary, Daddy." He didn't understand it and he didn't like the things that he saw. He was looking for me to tell him that he was going to be all right and that the war was going to stop. He was seven years old at the time and afraid because of what he was seeing (I was afraid too; it's just that adults are able to fake bravery a little better), and he wanted some answers. We need to be ready to incorporate what's happening in the world around us into our lessons and our prayers so that we can help children understand that God is their friend even when things are going wrong. Lessons are never taught in a vacuum; they must relate to life.

Each child's view of the world is different. Younger children view the world in terms of their room, house, apartment, neighborhood, and school. They don't understand much about the larger world. As children grow up they become more aware of the problems of politics, crime, war, global warming, and other global concerns through TV news, radio, magazines, and the movies. Teachers need to keep on top of the news and be ready to respond by incorporating current events into the lesson. (Try bringing a newspaper to your class every time you meet. It will provide you with lots of things for your class to discuss and pray about.) Giving students a chance to ask questions about things that are on their minds will give you the opportunity to help stu-

dents interpret what's happening in the light of God's Word.

Sometimes we will not always be completely prepared to do this if the event happens right before we are to teach the lesson, but usually we have more lead time than that.

Six Days between Lessons to Make Them Your Own

Sunday school teachers have a great advantage when it comes to making the lesson their own. They have six days to get their lesson together. The problem is that many Sunday school teachers do not know how to plan. See if you recognize the following scenario:

The Night Before the Morning to Come

Time: Any Saturday night from September through May, 10:43 p.m.

Setting: A kitchen table

Characters: A Sunday school teacher (starring you), a next-door neighbor, assorted members of the Sunday school teacher's family

Props: Sunday school lesson guide

The Scene Opens: You, the frenzied Sunday school teacher, have just finished giving a bath to your youngest child. Your sleeping spouse can be heard snoring in the bedroom. The older kids are watching a rerun of "Godzilla Meets Frankenstein" on the TV. It is now time for you to prepare for next morning's lesson: King David Brings the Ark of the Covenant into Jerusalem (2 Samuel 6). You quickly scan the materials needed for the lesson. They happen to include directions for making a tambourine out of paper plates and dried beans. "Directions: Take 10 dried beans and put them between two paper plates. Staple outside rim of paper plates together so that beans will not fall out. Shake tambourines at appropriate time during the dramatization of the story." That seems easy enough doesn't it? Now comes the hard part.

First you go to the cupboard to find the paper plates. Good—you bought the giant economy size last week at the store. You have 500 paper plates— no problem. You go to another cupboard to look for the dried beans and, much to your chagrin, there are no dried beans to be found. The time is now 10:57 p.m., and you are starting to suffer the first pangs of panic. You call your next door neighbor only to find that she too is out of beans (she has baked beans, French beans, and lima beans, but no dried beans). You look at the clock, grab your coat, and jump into the car (by now it's 11:01). There's still time to pick up the beans at the 24-hour convenience store. You are in luck—they have one package of dried beans left on the shelf.

Back at home (it's now 11:23 p.m.) you settle down to making one tambourine to show the class as an example. You have the plates, the beans, and your stapler. You put a few beans in the plate, put the other plate on top, and staple the edges. There are only two staples left in the stapler. It's now 11:30, and you still haven't really started to do what you need to do to teach the lesson.

The End.

Does this story sound just a little familiar? The last-minute preparation scenario is all too familiar, I'm afraid, for both experienced and inexperienced teachers. We all get caught in this situation when we haven't taken the time to prepare throughout the week. What I would like to do is give you some ideas about how you can avoid the preceding scenario through a 10-step process of pre-preparation.

Preparing Through Pre-Preparation

Step 1: Before you leave your classroom, you will have at least one idea about how you're going to teach your *next* lesson.

It is very important to know what's coming up next. It will not only influence what you are doing in your current lesson, but it will also start you thinking about how you're going to teach the next one. If you're teaching about David and the ark of the covenant today, it is important for you to be thinking about the David and Bathsheba story to be taught next week. Knowing what's next allows you to think about how you might teach the next story. It will give you the opportunity to ponder what materials and resources you might need to best teach the lesson. Before you leave your classroom you should have a good idea of what the next story is and have at least one idea about how you are going to teach it. The process of thinking ahead by at least one lesson will help you focus on a week-long series of steps that will get you ready to teach.

Step 2: When all the day's chores are done, take a few moments to look at the next lesson and read the Bible story.

As you read over any lesson, you naturally start to think about a variety of ways to teach it. But by looking at the lesson at the earliest possible moment, you will better be able to prepare yourself for teaching. Most importantly, you will be able to start making a list of the things that you need to do so that last-minute glitches will be minimized. I know it has probably been a long day for you, but take a few moments to get out your lesson books and glance over them.

Note: Sometimes you can look over a lesson while watching a football game on Sunday afternoon or Monday night. Actually any TV show will do, but football is probably the best kind of show to watch if you want to do lots of preparation. During a three-hour game you only see about 45 minutes of real action. The rest of the time is spent on commercials and endless babble by commentators. During these commercial down times you can get much of your lesson prepared. I'm not joking here—you really can take advantage of this down time to do lots of work. You can also use TV-watching time to do some of the tedious tasks that often accompany preparation of a lesson (making dried-bean tambourines, for example). As you glance over the upcoming lesson, you can make some notes regarding the materials that you will need to teach the lesson. P.S. If you miss a really good play, don't worry. You can always catch the instant replay.

Now this next part is very important. If you do nothing else, you must do this: Read the Bible story carefully. Read it at least once. Read it slowly and think through its plot, characters, setting, and theme. Jot down a few

important details. Note unfamiliar characters, vocabulary, geographic locations, and customs that are described in the text. These will be important as you continue your pre-preparation.

Step 3: Make sure that you have a copy of the Bible placed around the house at strategic locations.

A copy of the Bible should be handy in the following places:

1. Your bedroom night stand. I suggest that you place a copy of the Bible on your pillow after you make the bed. That way you will have to pick it up before you go to bed. Once you pick it up, you will have little trouble turning to the Bible story and reading it before you go to sleep each night. This suggestion is made for people who like to procrastinate. If your copy of the Bible is on your pillow, you will have a hard time ignoring it.

2. Next to your favorite easy chair

3. On your coffee table

4. In your study or library

5. In the family room or den

6. In the bathroom

My point is that we must avail ourselves of every opportunity to read the Scriptures for our personal study, edification, preparation and, yes, enjoyment. If we place copies of the Bible in a few strategic places in our homes, we will be more likely to pick them up and read them. If the Bible is found on the mantle, it is doubtful that we will take the time to walk over and pick it up. Reading the Bible should be habitual, but sometimes we need to help ourselves become better readers of the Word of God. This is especially true for people who have taken on the responsibility of teaching the faith to children.

Step 4: Use lots of translations and paraphrases of the Bible as you prepare.

You might also try reading the Bible story in several translations and paraphrases (*KJV, RSV, NIV, NET, LB, TEV*). By reading different translations you can gain new insights into the story, increase your understanding of difficult passages, and clarify vocabulary that is unfamiliar to you.

Whenever you sit down for serious preparation, you should probably have at least two translations of the Bible at hand—one which you can use as your primary source for study and another to act as a clarifier or expander for the story.

Step 5: On Monday, start to gather the books, puppets, flannelgraphs, maps, filmstrips, videotapes, adhesive tape, dried beans, paper plates, and staples that you will need for the lesson.

Don't get caught on Saturday night without your materials. Take the list of materials that you need for the lesson (which you made during the Vikings-Bears game on Sunday afternoon) and start to gather them. You may not collect all of them today, but you will at least make a dent in the list. As the week continues, pick up the rest of the things that you need. In any case, try to avoid "Saturday-night plight!"

Step 6: Preview and practice to insure a "glitch free" presentation.

As you gather the materials you will have a chance to do any previewing that is necessary. You can look through the filmstrips or video tape suggestions at your leisure and make notes to help you remember important ideas. Always preview. Never assume that you already know what's contained in prerecorded materials!

A teacher friend of mine once showed a movie to a class without previewing it. He just assumed that it was the right film because the title on the movie reel was the title that he had ordered. The film company had wound the wrong film on the reel. Much to his surprise, he started showing a movie about … well, I better not say. Let's just say he was more than slightly embarrassed.

When you have previewed the media, you will be able to discuss the key ideas with the students before they see or hear them. When students are alerted to the important vocabulary, characters, and ideas before they watch or listen to the media, they will understand and remember the contents of the media better.

Previewing also lets you find out if there are any glitches on the video, bad splices in the film, or scratches on the records. Glitches can make or break your day. By previewing you can correct them before you present them in class.

If you have selected a storybook to read to the children (an *Arch Book*[1] or a Bible story that has been retold by a noted children's author[2]) make sure that you practice reading it aloud at home before you read it to the class. If you have children at home, read it aloud to them. Practicing this way is like previewing—it lets you know where the glitches may be hiding. There's more to come on reading aloud in Chapter 3.

The same kind of practice holds true if you are using a flannelboard or a puppet to tell the story. Practice in front of a mirror so that you see what you look like or, if you can, try videotaping yourself.[3] You won't have to do this every time you teach, but you should do it at least once so you get an idea of what the children are seeing and hearing. Most people feel a little odd when they view themselves in the mirror or on TV. Don't let feeling odd stop you from doing something that will help you improve your ability to communicate more effectively with children.

Step 7: Sometime during the middle of the week, set aside time to do the bulk of your preparation.

Let's review what we are doing at this point for a moment. We have thought up at least one idea on how we are going to teach this week's lesson. Every day we are reading and rereading our Bible story. By the middle of the week we almost know it by heart. We have gathered and previewed all our materials and practiced any oral reading we might do. We have selected several translations of the Bible to study and are now ready to get down to serious, concentrated study and preparation of this week's lesson.

Set aside at least an hour for your lesson preparation. Go somewhere where you will not be disturbed. I know this is especially difficult for those of you who have small children, but this may be an opportunity for your

spouse to do something of great value. Baby-sitting for you as you do your lesson preparation is a most significant contribution to the mission of the church. This kind of service is not to be taken lightly. When a husband or wife helps their spouse to prepare to teach the faith, they are doing the good and gracious will of God. Husbands and wives should seriously discuss this time for preparation so that it can be done with a minimum of distraction and interruption. If preparation can only be done when the kids are all in bed, then preparation is likely to be done at the least productive time of the day. Try to think of ways to help your spouse find the quality time to prepare.

Step 8: Gather your power tools.

Once you've found a quiet place and time to prepare, you should surround yourself with the tools you need to do the job. The tools are books, and in a real sense, they are the power tools you need to get the job done. Some of them can be (like most power tools) expensive, but you don't have to acquire them all at one time. Many of them can be borrowed (just like drills and lawn mowers), and all can be given as Christmas, birthday, or Easter gifts. ("If you want to do the job you have to have the right tools. Then you can do the job right and do it quickly. If you don't have the right tools, you can bet you'll botch the job." Quote from my dad, a master carpenter and great teacher.)

Here is a brief list of basic power tools that every Sunday school teacher should have.

1. Bible dictionary

2. Any good dictionary of the English language (an important tool for any kind of study)

3. Bible maps or atlas

4. Several Bibles (including a study Bible in which you feel free to write and underline is a must)

5. A Bible commentary (some very good one- or two-volume commentaries are available)

6. A one-volume Bible encyclopedia

7. A concordance (Sometimes a good one is found in the back of a Bible, but a separate concordance is always a handy tool.)

(Fill in the blanks with your own "power tool" ideas)

8. _____

9. _____

10. _____

When you have the power tools together, you are ready to attack the lesson head on and to really prepare for the nitty-gritty of teaching. You will be set to do the kind of thorough, concentrated preparation, study, and reflection that leads to creative, enthusiastic teaching.

Step 9: Finalize the lesson.

Now it's time to get down to the final preparation of the lesson. Everything you have done so far has been pre-preparation. In the pre-prepa-

ration stage you have gathered various materials and thought about ways you might present the story that you are going to teach. To finalize the lesson you will need to carefully read the teacher's manual, review the biblical truths that are incorporated in the lesson, and outline it so that you will be able to make smooth transitions from opening devotions to closing activities. Take some time to figure out how you're going to distribute your materials, take attendance, collect offerings, etc. These little classroom management details can become big problems if they aren't carefully prepared.

Because you have done pre-preparation, you will be able to use the teachers guide more effectively. You won't have to spend time figuring out what the Bible story is about or worrying about where you will find the materials. You are now ready to effectively use the manual to guide you in the final preparation of your lesson.

I say *your* lesson, because by this time the lesson should be your own. You will have taken the lesson into your mind and heart before you read what someone else has said about how the lesson might be taught. Now that it's your own, you'll be better able to use the suggestions in the teachers guide and freely incorporate your own ideas as well. In this way you will be in a partner relationship with the author of the lesson. You will be able to speak to the teachers guide as opposed to merely listening to it.

If you've made the lesson your own, you may wish to change, expand, or leave out certain parts. You may find that you want to skip a lesson or two for some reason. If you do, someone might hit you with another killer phrase: "But don't we have to use everything? After all, we paid for it."

You and your faculty or staff will decide when you will skip some material to practice the Christmas service. You will decide when a field trip or visit to a hospital or nursing home will be substituted for a particular set of lessons. You will decide if a lesson best fits in your church-year calendar or whether a lesson should take two periods instead of one. In every case, it is **you** who will decide the appropriate ways to teach the lessons.

Step 10: Relax! Give yourself a reward!

If you have finalized your lesson by the middle of the week, you can relax. Well, almost. Because you have finalized the lesson early, you have the time to practice things that you feel still need to be strengthened (telling or reading the Bible story, writing an opening prayer or a devotion). You'll have two or three days in which to do any last minute polishing, but you will not have a panic attack on Saturday night. You can get a good night's sleep and be ready to teach the next day.

When you've finished your lesson preparation, give yourself a reward for a job well done. It doesn't have to be a big reward or something that's expensive, but it should be something that you enjoy. Maybe it will be as simple as promising yourself a piece of pie and ice cream when you finish your preparation. Maybe you will buy yourself a book or magazine that you want to read, or simply take a nap. Whatever reward you give yourself is okay as long as you have finished preparing. No cheating!

Of course the real reward of thorough preparation is good teaching. A well-taught lesson is its own reward.

This 10-step process will become easier to follow as time goes on. It is

a systematic (disciplined) way of approaching the teaching task. It provides one way to help you discipline yourself. There are many ways to approach the preparation of lessons, but I hope that these suggestions will help you think about how you prepare for teaching.

Teaching is a discipline—a self-discipline, if you will. By following a disciplined approach to your lesson preparation, you will find that the teaching will be easier and more enjoyable. Remember why you are preparing and how it will benefit the children you teach.

A Well-Prepared Teacher Is a Happy Teacher Because ...

There is another beneficial aspect to preparation. It cuts down on discipline problems. Preparation is the other essential ingredient that is necessary for effective discipline. When you have prepared thoroughly, your lesson will flow smoothly. Children know when teachers are underprepared. Children possess a sixth sense that automatically triggers a negative behavioral response. A prepared teacher is a happy teacher because thorough preparation breeds good discipline.

The essential ingredients in teaching are relationship, preparation, and discipline. They all effect one another and can't be separated. The equation looks like this:

Positive relationships with students and parents + A disciplined environment + Purposeful, prayerful preparation + God's blessings on our lessons through the Holy Spirit = A great lesson!

As you prepare for teaching the faith, you can do it with joy. Joy comes from the knowledge that God loves us and that we are his new creation in Christ Jesus. Joy-filled teaching is an expression of the love of God. As we teach we are modeling God's love to our students. They will see Jesus in us as we joyfully imitate him.

Jesus and Children

One day Jesus was surrounded by children. "People were bringing little children to Jesus to have him touch them, but the disciples rebuked them. When Jesus saw this, he was indignant. He said to them, 'Let the little children come to me, and do not hinder them, for the kingdom of God belongs to such as these' " (Mark 10:13–14).

Have you ever wondered why little children were surrounding Jesus? I think it was because he was a joy-filled person. Have you ever known parents to bring their children to someone who frowns, has a sour disposition, and never laughs? Would children want to be touched by someone like that? I don't think so. Jesus, the master teacher, was always prepared to meet children where they were and joyful to bless them.

Jesus models for us how we are to teach. "And he took the children in his arms, put his hands on them and blessed them" (Mark 10:16). As in the story of Jesus and the children, parents bring their children to us so that they can be touched by God through us. Parents want their children to be touched by the word of God. They want them to know that they are part of God's kingdom. They expect us to be faithful teachers and to help their children learn about God's plan of salvation. That's how Jesus touches chil-

dren today; he touches them through us.

When we teach about the mercies of God, we are taking children in our arms and blessing them. When we speak words of forgiveness and help children better understand their relationship with God, we are blessing them. When children are taught to pray and to praise and to give thanks to God for what he has done in Christ, they are blessed. As teachers we are Jesus' hands and feet, his voice and his arms. As we teach, we touch children with the words of God and, to our surprise, we are also blessed. When we teach others, we teach ourselves; when we feed others we also are fed. That's something to be joyful about.

A Joyful Teacher Prays*

Jesus, Master Teacher, Savior
Bless me as I teach today
Fill my teaching with your Spirit
Be my guide I humbly pray

Help my actions, words, and teaching
Be to ev'ry girl and boy
Signs that point them to your kingdom
Filled with love, grace, peace, and joy

Heav'nly Father Holy Spirit,
Jesus Christ, my dearest friend
Fill my teaching days with gladness
Joyful teaching without end.

* This prayer can also be sung to a hymn tune such as *Ringe richt,* "Sweet the Moments, Rich in Blessing" (*TLH* 155). You may wish to use this prayer/song at your next teachers meeting.

Something Else about the Way Jesus Taught

There's something else about the way Jesus taught that is important. Jesus loved to tell stories. To become like the master teacher we must also become master storytellers. Discipline, preparation, and relationships are all necessary for effective teaching, but you will still need to engage in ...

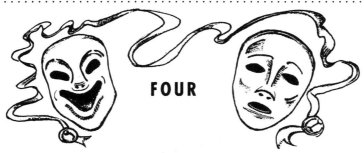

FOUR

Storytelling, Pantomimes, and Gospeldramas

Jesus was a masterful storyteller. Some of his stories are complex and symbolic; others are simple and straightforward. Jesus told stories loaded with action: A man goes from Jerusalem to Jericho and falls prey to thieves … a woman searches her house for a lost coin … laborers work all day in a vineyard … a sower sows seed that falls on rocky ground … a son squanders his inheritance on wild living. The parables of Jesus are filled with scenes that cry out to be dramatized. Our task as teachers of the faith is to look for new, dramatic ways to tell Bible stories to the children we teach.

When you finish this chapter, you'll be well on your way to being a writer, executive director, producer, key grip, actor, and storyteller *par excellence*. If this sounds a bit dramatic, it's meant to be. To be a good storyteller you have to be part actor, part director, part costume designer. As you read this chapter, you'll touch on a number of ideas and techniques that will call on your creative abilities as well as your organizational skills. Topics covered in this chapter:

1. Storytelling as a Dramatic Art

2. Storytelling Techniques:

    Echo Pantomimes

    Using a Script

    Story Reading

    Gospeldramas

Storytelling as a Dramatic Art

Jesus, the master storyteller, demonstrated that storytelling is a powerful teaching technique. Asked a question, Jesus often responded by telling a story (a parable) that cut to the heart of the matter. Jesus' stories not only instructed the listeners, they also prompted people to respond with questions and comments. Jesus knew that stories elicit a response from the audience; and a response is something every teacher wants from a child.

God has also given us the gifts, talent, creativity, and even the technology to tell Bible stories, the parables of Jesus, and the story of Christianity in new ways. Also, we have our own stories to tell, stories of our life experiences that can be used to supplement our lessons.

As you may have guessed by now, I love to tell stories. Storytelling is probably the most powerful way that we can express our deepest thoughts, memories, hopes, and dreams. Storytellers share their experiences with others, because they know that at the heart of their stories there lies a kernel of truth or an example to follow. Storytellers relate their experiences so that others can benefit from the wisdom found in the story.

To be a storyteller is to be an artist who paints word pictures in the mind of the listener. A good storyteller makes listeners feel they are really there; part of the action themselves. A teacher who is a good storyteller is a more effective teacher. A teacher who is a good storyteller will have more fun teaching.

Drama Means Action

Each story you tell must be dramatic; it must have action. The word *drama* literally means "to do." When you tell the story dramatically, it is assumed that you will "do" the story in a way that makes it *live* for the audience.

I hope that every teacher of the faith will be able to tell many types of action-filled stories. Here are some different types of stories that you can share with your students:

1. Stories about your own life

2. Stories about the lives of people whom you know personally (not gossip, but stories which come from your experience with others that will help to illustrate a truth)

3. Stories about people whom you have come to know through reading

4. Stories that you have heard others tell

5. Stories that you make up

6. Stories written by others that you read aloud dramatically

7. Stories from the Bible that you tell dramatically

8. Stories about faithful people of God (saints and martyrs and ordinary people of God who have extraordinary faith)

9. Stories about the history of the Christian church

10. Stories about the history of your local church

As an example, I would like to share a story with you from my own life. Please understand that a written story is much different than a spoken, live telling of a story. You can't see or hear the following: my gestures, the way I would walk, the inflections in my voice, the movements of my eyes and eyebrows, and other facial movements.

You will have to imagine my dramatic actions and "hear" my voice, for I "speak" to you through written words. Maybe you will try to tell or read this story to your class in a dramatic way and interpret my words using your own facial expressions, body movements, hand gestures, and voice inflections.

The following story is my own. It is true; it really happened to me.

I Call Someone a Name

In every neighborhood there is always one person all the children in the neighborhood seem to fear; a person who seems to have a perpetual

frown on their face and who yells at you if you ride your tricycle into their driveway. Our neighborhood had such a person. Her name was Mrs. Schradt, and she was very, very old. She walked a little stooped over as she shuffled down the street. Her voice was crackly and she spoke with a heavy German accent, which made her seem all the more mysterious. She always seemed to be looking at us out of the corners of her eyes, waiting for us to make a wrong move. Such was my perception of Mrs. Schradt when I was a 10-year-old.

One day I was playing catch with my friend from across the street. Mrs. Schradt and my friend's mom, Mrs. Gordon, were pals. It was not uncommon for Mrs. Schradt to go from house to house in the neighborhood and have a coffee klatch with her elderly neighbor friends. We kids could not understand why anyone would want to have coffee with Mrs. Schradt. What could they possibly talk about? Why did they bother? Didn't they know what a mean-spirited old lady she was? Such questions ran through our minds as we watched Mrs. Schradt hobble from house to house each afternoon.

In the middle of our game of catch, Mrs. Schradt came out the back door of Mrs. Gordon's house. The use of the front door (in our neighborhood) was restricted to formal occasions only. We heard the screen door bang shut and saw Mrs. Schradt advancing toward us right down the middle of the driveway. Why did she have to disturb our game? Couldn't she have gone down the side of the driveway? Nooo! Right down the middle of the drive she came like a juggernaut. We would either move aside or be crushed under her shuffling little feet. We moved aside. When she was well down the drive and out of sight, I leaned over to my friend and half whispered, "The old battle-ax." I had never used that expression before, and both my friend and I laughed under our breath at the aplomb with which I spoke the words. "The old battle-ax!" The words fell trippingly from my tongue. Didn't the expression fit the personality of this "catch game spoiler"?

We resumed our game for a few more minutes, until my friend was called into the house for supper. When I got home, I found my mom and grandma sitting at the kitchen table with their arms folded in front of them. Steaming cups of coffee sat on the kitchen table as I entered the back door and took off my shoes. In our house you always took your shoes off in the kitchen. My mom looked at me with that look that only mothers can conjure and said, "What did you call Mrs. Schradt?"

There was ice in her words as she spoke them. I glanced at Grandma for help, but she only stared me down with a stoic face that confirmed that I had had it. My mom's words still echoed in my ears "What did you call Mrs. Schradt … Schradt … Schradt … ?"

"Why did she bother asking me," I thought. Mrs. Schradt had obviously been there and told them the whole sordid account. I never had a chance to answer. "You go right over to Mrs. Schradt's house and apologize to her this minute!" said my mom.

Mrs. Schradt's house was next door to our house, only a few yards as the crow flies. To get there would take only a few seconds by the direct route. At this time, however, I decided to take the scenic route which lead down our driveway to the street and then up the Schradt's driveway. This route was three times the distance.

Looking back on this event I am still amazed that, for the first time, I took an interest in the flora and fauna of my neighborhood. I stopped to examine stones on the ground.

"Are these igneous or metamorphic?" I mused as I stooped to pick up these heretofore uninteresting stones. I looked at a gray squirrel that I had seen so many times before with the scrutinizing eye of a biologist who is about to discover a new species. In other words, I did anything to stall the inevitable.

One can only stall so long. Eventually, like my grandpa used to say, "You've got to face the music." As I approached the front door of the house (I went to the front door because I figured this was a formal occasion), I began to get that sickening feeling that you get in your stomach when you know you have been caught in the act. The screen door with the big aluminum letter "S" loomed before me as I put out my finger and touched the doorbell. I thought that if the doorbell wasn't working, I could go home and tell Mom and Grandma that I rang, but nobody answered the door. I wasn't that lucky. Through the squiggly glass next to the door I saw the shadowy figure of Mrs. Schradt creeping toward me. As she opened the big oak door it squeaked like the door on the old "Inner Sanctum" radio show. Errrrrrrrrrrr, went the door. By now I was petrified.

She opened the screen door and stood in front of me—all 93 pounds of her. At my ripe old age of 10 years I was only tall enough to look her right in the eyes. She said nothing, but merely stared me down waiting for me to speak.

Then a terrible thing happened. I'm sure that this has happened to you in similar circumstances. I started to cry. Not the boo-hoo kind of crying that we all have seen accompanied by crocodile tears, but the kind of crying that sounds like this: haaaaaaaa, catch a quick breath, haaaaaaaaa, try to catch another breath, haaaaaaaaa. With real tears welling in my eyes I said, with quivering voice: "Mrs. Schradt—haaaaa (catch a breath) Schradt. I'mmmm sorry that, haaaaaa (catch a breath) that I called you a, haaaaaaa, bat—tle, haaaaa, axe, haaaaaa! Can yooou forgivehaaaaaaa, m-me!?"

Mumbling words like these between sobs and tears and haaaaaaaaa's of guilt, fear, and embarrassment was no small thing for me to do. I remember it as if it were happening right now and can almost feel what happened next. Mrs. Schradt came toward me, her gnarled hands stretching out in front of her. She put her arms around me and gave me a strong hug. I didn't think that she had that much strength in her. Then, while holding me as tightly as she could, she whispered these German accented words into my ear: "Dat's all right, Cheffrey, I forgiff you."

Then she looked at me and smiled. "Thank you, Mrs. Schradt," I said as I wiped the tears out of my eyes.

"Dat's okay. You go home now qvick—und don't vorry abow dit," Mrs. Schradt said as she shooed me back to my house.

I ran back home—actually I flew. The world was mine! I had experienced something wonderful. I had been forgiven. I asked her to forgive me and she did. This was the first time in my life that I can remember confessing a sin and being absolved by someone outside my family. It left a lasting

impression on me—I think that I'm a better forgiver because of it. It also taught me something about the lady whom I had slandered and disliked. I found out that she was a caring person who could forgive and forget.

I often think of Mrs. Schradt and the great gift of forgiveness that she gave me. She used the peculiar power which Christ has given to his people. He has given us the power to forgive one another. When Mrs. Schradt said "I forgiff you," it was as if Christ himself had said it. I thank God for Mrs. Schradt and all the other people who have forgiven me when I have sinned against them.

The End.

Such is my story. I hope that you can relate to it (or maybe found some of yourself in it). If you want to read it aloud to your class when you discuss sin and forgiveness, please feel free to do so. What I really want you to do, however, is to tell your own stories. The children will listen and understand because they are real and come from your own experience. They are your own life's drama.

Good storytellers do more than tell; they analyze and amplify. Here is the same story I just told you presented in a different way:

When I was 10, I called a lady in my neighborhood a nasty name. When I apologized to her, she forgave me. The End.

I think that you can see the difference. Storytellers must tell their stories in dramatic, interesting, and enthusiastic ways. The audience must feel that they are living the story with the storyteller.

In order to tell the story dramatically, you must analyze and amplify each facet of the story. That doesn't mean that you fabricate something that didn't happen. You amplify it by explaining it in descriptive ways so that the listeners get the "you are there" feeling.

This careful analysis and amplification applies to stories from the Bible as well as to personal stories. A careful analysis of the story will enable you to add the dramatic "bits of business" that make stories come alive for the listener. To do this you must be aware of your facial expressions, eye contact, gestures, vocal inflections, accents, costumes, props, makeup, lighting, classroom atmosphere, and audience reactions.

That's a pretty long list, but attending to as many details as you can will make the difference between merely *talking through* the story and *dramatically telling* it. What makes storytelling different from watching TV or going to the movies is its "living" nature. When you tell a story "live," you do it in relationship to a living, breathing, responsive audience. The audience reactions will make a difference to you in the way you tell the story. By noting the audience reactions you will know when to pause, to move, to be emphatic, and to whisper.

There are many storytelling techniques that help the audience participate in the story. I would like to concentrate on four types of storytelling techniques: 1) Echo pantomimes; 2) Telling stories without a script; 3) Story reading; 4) Storytelling through what I call Gospeldramas.

Storytelling Techniques

Echo Pantomimes

One of the most engaging dramatic techniques for telling stories is the echo pantomime. An echo pantomime contains three elements: 1) a story is broken down into simple, short sentences or phrases; 2) each sentence is accompanied with a simple, appropriate action; 3) each sentence and action is repeated by the audience. Here is a short example that demonstrates the echo pantomime technique:

The Storyteller	*The Audience*
The storyteller says:	The audience says:
1. Hello! (*waves hand in "hello" gesture*)	1. Hello! (*they imitate the "hello" wave*)
2. Are you feeling good? (*makes a muscle with both arms*)	2. Are you feeling good? (*make "muscles" with both arms*)
3. Yes, I am! (*nods head yes*)	3. Yes, I am! (*nod heads yes*)
4. Good! (*thumbs up gesture*)	4. Good! (*thumbs up*)
5. Would you like to hear a story? (*cup hands around both ears*)	5. Would you like to hear a story? (*cup hands around both ears*)
6. Well, here it is. (*extend both hands with palms up in giving gesture*)	6. Well, here it is. (*extend hands in giving gesture with palms up*)
Then on you go with the story …	

You can use this kind of introduction to demonstrate how the echo pantomime is done. Echo pantomimes can be used with a wide range of age groups. Remember that younger children cannot follow or repeat complex sentences and gestures. Keep them simple for the little children, but don't be afraid to get more complex as you do them with older children and adults. That's right—adults should do the echo pantomimes right along with the children. Echo pantomimes are excellent ways to dramatize Bible stories and make scripture lessons come alive.

Echo pantomimes need no rehearsal on the part of the audience, but must be carefully constructed and practiced by the storyteller/mime. As you read on, you will find three examples of echo pantomimes that I have written for different occasions. I'll explain how they were written and give you some practice at writing one or two yourself.

How to Write a Simple Echo Pantomime

A few years ago I was asked to dramatize the Gospel lesson from Mark 7:31–37 (the healing of a deaf and mute man). I thought that an echo pantomime would be an appropriate way to help young children understand the story and to involve the congregation in an active way. Here's how I went about writing the echo pantomime.

1. I broke the passage into short sentences and "translated" them into short phrases that could easily be acted out or mimed.

"Then Jesus left the vicinity of Tyre and went through Sidon, down to the Sea of Galilee and into the region of the Decapolis." Translation: "One day, Jesus was out for a walk."

"There some people brought to him a man who was deaf and could hardly talk, and they begged him to place his hand on the man." Translation: "Some people brought a man to Jesus. The man couldn't hear. And he could hardly speak. They wanted Jesus to touch the man."

"Then he spit and touched the man's tongue." Translation: "Jesus touched the man's tongue." (Note: I have left out the spitting part, because this could be a problem for overzealous children who sometimes take the pantomime a little too literally.)

"He looked up to heaven and with a deep sigh said to him, *'Ephphatha!' (Ephphatha* means 'Be opened!')" Translation: "Jesus looked up to heaven. He took a deep breath and said, 'Open up!' "

(At this point I'm going to ask a question that is not found in the passage. Storytellers have the dramatic license to occasionally ask a question of the audience or make a comment on the action. Questions and comments help the audience focus on what is happening or what might happen next.)

"And do you know what?"

"At this, the man's ears were opened, his tongue was loosened, and he began to speak plainly." Translation: "The man could hear. And the man could speak as plain as day."

"Jesus commanded them not to tell anyone." Translation: "Jesus said, 'Let's keep this a secret.' "

"But the more he did so, the more they kept talking about it." Translation: "But nobody could."

"People were overwhelmed with amazement." Translation: "They were all amazed!"

" 'He has done everything well,' they said." Translation: "They said, 'He does everything well!' "

" 'He even makes the deaf hear and the mute speak.' " Translation: " 'He makes deaf people hear! And tongue-tied people speak!' "

2. I put actions together with the rewritten words.

Once the "translation" is complete, actions needed to be added to them. The actions I chose are printed below, but, if you choose to use them, they still need to be interpreted. Or, feel free to substitute actions of your own that may work better for you. Practice reading the echo pantomime a few times before you add the actions to the words.

Hint: After you develop your own echo pantomime, print it on a large piece of paper or poster board that can be read from a few feet away. That way, you won't have to be worried about memorizing it. In addition, you might want to highlight in some way the individual words you want to emphasize.

I usually like to do an echo pantomime from a raised platform (a choir conductor's podium is a good thing to use) or a wooden box. That way, the audience can easily see the actions. I also use a music stand to hold the script because, unlike a lectern, it doesn't block the view of the audience. Don't be afraid to speak loud and to stand up and do the actions.

At the end of the story here, I have added a doxology (praise to the Father, Son, and Holy Spirit). I always like to let the people know in whose name we are doing the story.

(See Echo Pantomine at right.)☛

You will have to repeat the gestures and words a few times to coordinate them. You won't get it "perfect" right away, but with a little trial and error, you'll be ready for an Oscar award. Try it out at home with your children (I always do) to work out the kinks.

Write an Echo Pantomime Yourself

What comes next is a sample story for you to script in echo-pantomime style. Analyze it by taking each sentence of the story and simplifying it. Write a "translation" and appropriate actions to accompany the words in the blanks.

Step 1—Carefully read the story.

Jesus Walks on the Water (Matthew 14:22–33)

Immediately Jesus made the disciples get into the boat and go on ahead of him to the other side, while he dismissed the crowd. After he had dismissed them, he went up on a mountainside by himself to pray. When evening came, he was there alone, but the boat was already a considerable distance from land, buffeted by the waves because the wind was against it. During the fourth watch of the night Jesus went out to them, walking on the lake. When the disciples saw him walking on the lake, they were terrified. "It's a ghost," they said, and cried out in fear. But Jesus immediately said to them: "Take courage! It is I. Don't be afraid." "Lord, if it is you, Peter replied "tell me to come to you on the water." "Come," he said. Then Peter got down out of the boat, walked on the water, and came toward Jesus. But when he saw the wind, he was afraid and, beginning to sink, cried out "Lord, save me!" Immediately Jesus reached out his hand and caught him. "You of little faith," he said, "why did you doubt?" And when they climbed into the boat the wind died down. Then those who were in the boat worshiped him, saying "Truly you are the Son of God."

Although I printed out here only the Matthew account, Mark and John record it as well. It's good to read the different tellings for several reasons:

The Healing of a Deaf and Mute Man: An Echo Pantomime

(A welcome or introduction to the echo pantomime can be done here if you desire.)

One day,

(Point index finger of right hand to sky)

Jesus was out for a walk.

(Walk in place)

Some people brought a man to see Jesus.

(Hold both hands out, palms up, and pull them toward you)

They wanted Jesus to touch the man.

(Point to audience with right hand, then touch your left hand with your right hand)

The man couldn't hear,

(Cover your ears with your hands)

and he could hardly speak.

(Cross your hands in front of your mouth)

Jesus touched the man's tongue.

(Wiggle fingers of both hands in front of your mouth)

Jesus looked up to heaven,

(Look up)

he took a deep breath,

(Take a quick breath)

and said, "Open up!"

(Make opening gesture toward the sky with both hands)

And do you know what?

(At the words "you," "know," and "what," point three times to three locations in the audience)

The man could hear!

(Cup hands behind ears)

And the man could speak as plain as day.

(Cup hands around mouth in megaphone gesture)

Jesus said, "Let's keep this a secret."

(Put index finger in front of mouth, the "keep it quiet" gesture)

But nobody could.

(Shake head no)

They were all

(Sweeping gesture across whole audience)

amazed.

(Put hand above head and shake hands quickly)

They said, "He does everything well.

(Both hands make "thumbs up" gesture on the word everything)

He makes deaf people hear

(Hands cupped over ears and opened up on word hear)

and tongue-tied people speak."

(Hands in front of mouth and opened in "megaphone" gesture on the word speak)

All praise to the Father;

(Right hand index finger points to the sky)

all praise to the Son;

(Point down toward the horizon)

all praise to the Spirit—

(Make "sign of the cross" gesture by pointing from left to right)

three

(Hold up three fingers pointing to the sky)

in one!

(Point with index finger to the sky)

1. It helps in understanding the story better.

2. Some details may be in one account that are not in another.

3. Reading the story several times helps memory.

4. One translation may be easier to dramatize than another.

In particular, you may want to refer to *A Synopsis of the Gospels: The Synoptic Gospels with Johannine Parallels,* by H. F. D. Sparks (Fortress Press, 1964). This book lets you see all four Gospel accounts at one time; it shows each of the gospel texts in side-by-side columns for easy comparison. The word *synoptic* means "seeing together" (*syn*=together; *optic*=see). The gospels of Matthew, Mark, and Luke are called the synoptic gospels because they tell the stories of our Savior's life in a similar way and in pretty much the same order. The gospel of John tells and "sees" the stories from a different viewpoint than the synoptics. When you can read all the accounts in parallel, you will be able to retell the story in greater detail as you write your own echo pantomimes. (Also see *The Parallel Bible.*)

The other translations I use most of the time are the *Oxford Annotated Bible* (RSV), *Good News for Modern Man,* and *The New English Bible.* You don't have to use this many versions when you do your writing, but I have found them helpful.

It's also extremely helpful to use other reference tools to help you write. I would like to suggest a few of them and briefly comment about how they are useful. (See the list of reference and teaching tools found on pages 148–152 for additional resources.)

1. The *Concordia Self-Study Bible* (New International Version). This study Bible is filled with notes, color atlas, black and white illustrations and diagrams, time lines, cross references, concordance, indexes, summaries, and outlines of every book, and other helps. I highly recommend this edition of the Bible to you. Incidentally, on pages 1488–90 you will find an outline of the entire life of Christ.[1] If you have ever forgotten where the story of "Jesus visits Mary and Martha" is, a glance at these pages will tell you. If you want to find where a particular miracle is found (in any of the Gospels), you need only glance at this outline. From Concordia Publishing House, 1986, $39.95—and worth every penny. (PS: The story of Mary and Martha is found in Luke 10:38–42.)

2. The *Concordia Self-Study Commentary.* After I read a Bible story, I always like to read a commentary on it. This one-volume commentary on the whole Bible will help you study the Scriptures and give you insight into unfamiliar passages, customs, and vocabulary. From Concordia Publishing House, 1979, $26.95—for 950 pages; that's less than three cents a page!

3. A Bible dictionary. Any Bible dictionary will be helpful to you in understanding the vocabulary, artifacts, and customs contained in Scripture. I recently bought the *Harper's Bible Dictionary* (Harper and Row Publishers, 1985, $37.95) and found it to be a good addition to my theological library. It also contains numerous pictures and illustrations valuable to teachers.

4. I also use Bible encyclopedias and handbooks as reference tools when I write my echo pantomimes, and Gospeldramas. (See the reference section for a selection).

Step 2—Set the stage with an introduction.

Introduce your echo pantomime with a brief statement that "sets the stage" for the audience. For example, you could relate what has come before the story so that the audience has an idea of when and where the story takes place. If you have your Bible handy, you will notice that Jesus has just finished feeding the 5,000. He tells his disciples to get in the boat and go to the other side of the lake while he dismisses the crowd. Then Jesus takes time to be alone and pray before he meets up with the disciples.

Here is a possible introduction that you might use:

> Right after Jesus had fed the 5,000 people, he told his disciples that they should get into a boat and go to the other side of the lake while he dismissed the crowd. After the people were gone, Jesus went up on a mountainside where he could be by himself to pray. When evening came, Jesus was alone and the boat with the disciples was a long way from the shore. And now, our story begins. You repeat my words and actions as we tell the story: "Jesus Walks on the Water."

Step 3—Break the story into short sentences or phrases. Write out the actions.

Below, I've broken the passage into short phrases for you, but you may wish to break them differently. (Remember to compare Mark's and John's accounts.) As you fill in the "actions" blanks, remember four things: 1) keep the actions simple; 2) try them out before you write them down; 3) do them slowly to make sure that they will work; and 4) exaggerate your actions so that your audience can easily see and follow them.

Keep in mind that there are many ways the story can be told and many actions that can accompany the words. No one way is right or wrong. Let your own sense of drama be your guide.

During the fourth watch of the night [i.e., between 3:00 and 6:00 a.m.]

(words) _____

(actions) _____

Jesus went out to them,

(words) _____

(actions) _____

walking on the lake.

(words) _____

(actions) _____

When the disciples saw him walking on the lake,

(words) _____

(actions) _____

they were terrified.

(words) _____

(actions) _____

"It's a ghost," they said,

(words) _____

(actions) _____

and cried out in fear.

(words) _____

(actions) _____

But Jesus immediately said to them:

(words) _____

(actions) _____

"Take courage!"

(words) _____

(actions) _____

"It is I.

(words) _____

(actions) _____

Don't be afraid."

(words) _____

(actions) _____

"Lord, if it is you,"

(words) _____

(actions) _____

Peter replied,

(words) _____

(actions) _____

"tell me to come to you

(words) _____

(actions) _____

on the water."

(words) _____

(actions) _____

"Come," he said.

(words) _____

(actions) _____

Then Peter got down out of the boat,

(words) _____

(actions) _____

walked on the water,

(words) _____

(actions) _____

    and came toward Jesus.

(words) _____

(actions) _____

    But when he saw the wind,

(words) _____

(actions) _____

    he was afraid and,

(words) _____

(actions) _____

    beginning to sink,

(words) _____

(actions) _____

    cried out,

(words) _____

(actions) _____

    "Lord, save me!"

(words) _____

(actions) _____

    Immediately Jesus reached out his hand

(words) _____

(actions) _____

    and caught him.

(words) _____

(actions) _____

    "You of little faith," he said,

(words) _____

(actions) _____

    "why did you doubt?"

(words) _____

(actions) _____

    And when they climbed into the boat

(words) _____

(actions) _____

    the wind died down.

(words) _____

(actions) _____

Then those who were in the boat worshiped him,

(words) _____

(actions) _____

saying "Truly you are the Son of God."

(words) _____

(actions) _____

Various Ways to Perform the Script

Some echo pantomimes are relatively complex and will take some rehearsal. In some respects, they can become like playlets. Don't let a complex story deter you. You have permission to tell the story whichever way you think will best suit your audience and your resources.

Here are a few suggestions for performing a complex echo pantomime:

1. Break longer, more complex echo pantomimes into two or three smaller acts. Each act can be performed by a different narrator or cast as the case may be. If you break it up into two or three acts, it might be a good idea to start each with a little recap of what went before or, simply read the last two lines of the preceding act so that you get a running start into the next act.

2. Each line or sentence of the story can be spoken by a different narrator/mime. For example, if you are performing it in a church setting, half of the audience could follow someone on the pulpit side while the other half follows someone on the lectern side. This alternating action gives half the audience a little rest while the other half follows the actions and words. For a short echo pantomime, each child can be given a line or two to say and act out with the audience.

3. Have the audience watch a performance group do the echo pantomime. (The audience might be the congregation, or you might have older students perform for younger ones.)

For example, perform the pantomime as a drama in which actors mime as a narrator reads the story line. Sometimes it is good to hide the narrator from the sight of the audience so that they can focus their eyes completely on the mime(s) while listening to the story. Use a microphone for the narrator so he or she can easily be heard.

4. Several narrators can be used to speak different parts of the story (assign one as narrator, one as the angel, one as Jesus).

5. Perform the echo pantomime with puppets, flannelgraphs, paper cut-outs, or other visual media.

Here is a relatively complex pantomime you may wish to adapt to your situation. Feel free to modify and recreate the pantomime in the dramatic form which you think will work best for you. As you prepare for this echo pantomime, take the time to highlight words that you think should be emphasized, and modify any lines and actions so that they work best for you. (Hint: I've numbered the lines so that, if you want to rehearse a certain section, you can simply say, "Let's take it from [e.g.] line 16.")

Easter Morning: An Echo Pantomime based on the Four Gospels

1. Early on Sunday morning
   (Open hands like sunrise)

2. while it was still dark,
   (Cover eyes with hands)

3. Mary Magdalene,
   (Hands point to one side)

4. Mary the Mother of James,
   (Hands point to the other side)

5. and some other women
   (Open hands to audience)

6. who were friends of Jesus
   (Clasp hands)

7. brought spices to his tomb.
   (Hands open and outstretched)

8. They were going to put the spices on the body of Jesus.
   (One hand palm up while the other hand moves to it in touching gesture)

9. They were very sad.
   (Head bows slightly while hands go to eyes in crying gesture)

10. As they walked,
    (Walk in place)

11. they were worried about
    (Hands on cheeks)

12. who would roll the great big stone
    (Hands do rolling gesture)

13. away from the tomb.
    (Both hands push out toward audience)

14. All of a sudden
    (Hands up quickly)

15. the ground began to shake,
    (Stamp feet)

16. and from up in the sky
    (Point up to sky—look up)

17. an angel came down
    (Hand comes down)

18. as white as lightning.
    (Hands palms up shade eyes)

19. And the angel rolled the stone away
    (Hands in rolling gesture)

20. and sat on the stone.
    (Bend knees slightly)

21. The soldiers guarding the tomb
    (Salute)

22. shook with fear
    (Clench hands and shake)

23. and fainted dead away.
    (Close eyes and tilt head to side)

(Here might be a place to break for Act II. You could sing a stanza of a hymn as an interlude.)

24. The women went into the tomb.
    (Walk in place with head and shoulders shrunk in fear)

25. They were amazed
    (Hands palms up shake hands)

26. and puzzled
    (Scratch head)

27. and afraid.
    (Cower)

28. But the angel said,
    (Index finger points up)

29. "Don't be amazed
    (Shake head in "no" gesture)

30. or puzzled
    (Scratch head)

31. or afraid.
    (Cower and shake)

32. I know whom you're looking for.
    (Index finger points to head)

33. You're looking for Jesus,
    (Index finger points to the sky)

34. who was crucified.
    (Hands form a cross)

35. You won't find him here.
    (Shake head while index fingers point to ground)

36. Remember what he said:
    (Index finger taps forehead)

37. He was going to be crucified,
    (Hands form a cross)

38. and on the third day
    (Hold up three fingers)

39. he would rise from the dead."
    (Both hands raise up—palms up)

40. And do you know what happened then?
    (Both hands spread open toward audience)

41. They remembered
    (Index finger taps forehead)

42. what Jesus had said.
    (Index finger points up)

43. And they ran out of the tomb
    (Run in place)

44. and trembled with fear
    (Tremble with hands clenched)

45. and trembled with joy.
    (Hands fly up and open)

46. And when they turned to leave,
    (Turn body slightly)

47. Jesus appeared before them
    (Open hands, palms up, to audience)

48. and said,
    (One hand up, with palm to audience)

49. "All hail. Hello."
    (Wave hand)

(This might be a place to break for Act II if you like.)

50. And they all fell down on their knees
    (Bend knees)

51. and worshiped at his feet.
    (Praying hands and bow head)

52. Then Jesus said, "Go and tell all my disciples
    (One hand sweeps slowly from left to right)

53. they will see me soon."
    (Hands make binoculars around eyes)

54. And the women turned around
    (Turn body around)

55. and ran as fast
    (Run in place)

56. as their legs would carry them.
    (Put hands on legs)

57. And they told the disciples
    (Cup hands in front of mouth)

58. what they had seen
    (Hands make binoculars)

59. and heard.
    (Cup hands by ears)

60. But some disciples shook their heads
    (Shake head in no gesture)

61. and folded their arms and said,
    (Fold arms)

62. "We don't believe you."
    (With arms folded shake head no)

63. But Peter got up,
    (Unfold arms, stand straight up)

64. and John got up,
    (Jump up slightly)

65. and they ran to the tomb.
    (Run in place)

66. And they looked inside,
    (Hand over forehead in "look" gesture)

67. but Jesus wasn't there.
    (Look at audience and shake head no)

68. After awhile
    (Tilt head)

STORYTELLING, PANTOMIMES, AND GOSPELDRAMAS 53

69. they went away
(Slow walk in place)

70. wondering what had happened.
(Scratch head while slowly walking)

71. But you know
(Point to audience)

72. and I know
(Point to self)

73. exactly what happened.
(Both hands palms up toward audience)

74. Jesus,
(Fold hands)

75. the Son of God,
(Raise folded hands)

76. who was crucified,
(Hands out to side)

77. died,
(Bow head)

78. and was buried in a tomb,
(One hand covers the other)

79. rose from the dead!
(Both hands up and extended out)

(Note that the following section is done in rhyme.)

80. This is the story;
(Index finger points up)

81. we know it is true.
(Point to head and shake head yes)

82. Because Jesus rose,
(Both hands raise up)

83. we all shall rise too.
(Sweep audience with hand)

84. For nothing from birth
(Shake head no, move hands no)

85. 'til we breathe our last breath
(Hands out palms up)

86. shall separate us
(Hands push away)

87. from his life-giving death.
(Hands out to sides)

88. For each of us died
(Point to each member of audience)

89. in Baptism's flood,
(Hands together and out quickly)

90. And each of us rise
(Point to each)

91. in his body and blood.
(Point to sky **or** gesture toward altar)

92. Remember the story;
(Touch forehead with finger)

93. believe it is true;
(Cross hands on chest and nod "yes")

94. because Jesus arose,
(Hands gesture up, palms up)

95. we all shall rise too.
(Hands outstretched to audience)

96. So praise to the Father,
(Point to the sky)

97. and praise to the Son,
(Point down to earth)

98. and praise to the Spirit—
(Complete sign of the cross)

99. the great Three-In-One!
(Point to sky with three fingers and then index finger)

Storytelling without Using a Script

So far the stories that I have told you have relied on scripts. They were carefully written and, to a great extent, were intended to be read word-for-word by the storyteller or actor(s).

It is important that you also develop the ability to tell stories without a script. To do this, you must overcome the natural fear that you will forget to say something important or that what you say off the top of your head is going to sound confused, inarticulate, and jumbled.

First of all, when telling a Bible story, you are probably not going to be telling it off the top of your head. If you have read the story several times and made it your own (as described in Chapter 2), you will know the story very well. If you know the major elements of the plot, characters, and setting of the story, you are ready to tell the story without a script. Here are some suggestions on how to go about it.

Memorize Only Key Material

Many people think that memorizing will allow them to tell the story well. Indeed, there are times when you may wish to memorize a story or have it memorized well enough that you need only refer to the text occasionally. For most purposes, however, you will not have time to memorize an entire story.

Consider memorizing key passages or phrases of the story—those passages so important that everyone should hear the exact words. When a line worthy of being memorized comes up (e.g., Moses: "Let my people go!"; Jesus: "Blessed are they who have not seen and yet have believed."; Thomas: "My Lord and my God."), it's important for the storyteller to know it by heart.

When storytellers memorize key passages, they model memorization for their students. If you expect that your students memorize Bible passages, you must show them that you think it is important for yourself as well. More on this when we get to the chapter on memorization.

Break the Story into Episodes

Feel free to use note cards or cue cards (large cue cards that can be read from a distance are great helps). Make sure that you outline; don't scrunch a 500-word script on your 5 × 8 note cards. Here's an example of the kind of outline that you might use to tell a Bible story. Start by reading the account of the "Temptation of Jesus" (Matthew 4:1–11, *RSV*).

> Then Jesus was led by the Spirit into the wilderness to be tempted by the devil. And he fasted forty days and forty nights, and afterward he was hungry. And the tempter came and said to him "If you are the Son of God, command these stones to become loaves of bread." But he answered "It is written, 'Man shall not live by bread alone, but by every word that proceeds from the mouth of God.' " Then the devil took him to the holy city, and set him on the pinnacle of the temple, and said to him, "If you are the Son of God, throw yourself down; for it is written, 'He will give his angels charge of you,' and 'On their hands they will bear you up, lest you strike your foot against a stone.' " Jesus said to him, "Again it is written, 'You shall not tempt the Lord your God.' " Again, the devil took him to a very high mountain, and

showed him all the kingdoms of the world and the glory of them; and he said to him, "All these I will give you, if you will fall down and worship me." Then Jesus said to him, "Begone, Satan! for it is written, 'You shall worship the Lord your God and him only shall you serve.' " Then the devil left him, and behold, angels came and ministered to him.

This passage could be broken down into a few episodes and outlined as follows:

The Temptation of Jesus—Outline

I. Introduction: Jesus led by Spirit into wilderness. The purpose: to be tempted by the devil.

    A. Fasting: 40 days/40 nights

    B. Jesus was hungry.

II. Tempter comes for first time.

    A. Tempter tempts Jesus with "stones to bread" idea.

    B. Jesus: "Man does not live by bread alone, but on every word that comes from the mouth of God." (Memorize this quote.)

III. Devil comes for second time.

    A. Devil takes Jesus to the high point of the temple.

    B. Devil says: "Throw yourself down."

    C. Jesus: "Do not put the Lord your God to the test" (memorize).

IV. Devil comes a third time.

    A. Devil takes Jesus to a high mountain.

    B. Devil shows Jesus all the kingdoms of the world and all the glory in them.

    C. Devil says that he will give all this to Jesus if "you fall down and worship me."

    D. Jesus responds: "Begone, Satan! for it is written, 'You shall worship the Lord your God and him only shall you serve' " (memorize).

V. The devil leaves and angels minister to Jesus.

This sample outline has more than enough information to tell the story. Now it's a matter of telling the story in your own words and filling in the dramatic details.

Picture the Action in Your Mind

Once you have your outline, it's time to picture each episode or event in your mind. Imagine what each episode "looks like," and then explain each in order. The story of the temptation of Jesus can be broken into several episodes, for example:

I.   Introduction

II.   Stones to bread

III.   Heights of the temple

IV.   The High Mountain;

V.   Angels attend Jesus.

Then use the following steps as you tell the story.

1. Imagine each of these episodes in your mind's eye for a moment right now. Take them one at a time.

2. As you picture each of these episodes, ask yourself, "What will I say in each episode? What details will I add? What gestures will I use? Are there any props or pictures I can use to tell the story?"

3. Now go back to the outline and tell the story aloud as you think through each scene. Use as many gestures as you can to help you act out the words (your actions will help you to remember what to say). Use a audiocassette tape recorder to record what you say so that you can listen to yourself later. Listening to yourself a few times will help you to improve your storytelling technique and help you to review and remember the story.

4. Review the Bible text and your outline to see if you have forgotten any important parts. By breaking the big story into a series of small episodes, you will be less intimidated by the size of the big story and be able to tell it with a greater degree of comfort.

Use Props and Pictures to Tell the Story

Once you have broken the story into its component parts, you can attach a picture or a prop to each part. The picture or prop will help you remember both the order of the episodes and the details that are necessary to make the story come alive.

Pictures of the story can be drawn on the chalkboard or on paper, and props can be shown in proper sequence. The pictures and props will serve to outline the story for you. For example, here is how you might tell the story of the "Temptation of Jesus."

Picture:

Jesus led by the Spirit into the wilderness.

Picture:

Jesus fasted for 40 days and nights.

Prop:

Stones

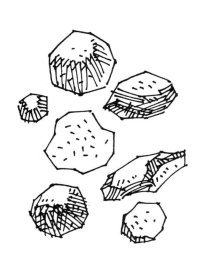

Prop:

A piece of bread

Jesus said, "Man does not live by bread alone …."

Picture:

Jesus telling the devil, "Don't put God to the test!"

Picture:

Mountain with Jesus and devil. Satan saying, "All this I give to you." Jesus responds, "Away from me, Satan."

Picture:

The temple and city below

Picture:

Angels

Prop:

One large stone

Picture:

Angels minister to Jesus

These seven simple pictures and three props form an outline that will help you to remember the story and tell it dramatically. Pictures and props are powerful visual stimuli that help students focus their attention on the story being told. And, you can refer back to the pictures and props as you review the story with the class. They also serve as reminders for the students as you continue to teach the lesson after telling the story. And, finally, they can also help students tell or retell the story to their classmates.

Here's how the story could be told using the pictures, props, and gestures. The <u>underlined words</u> indicate words that could be memorized by the storyteller. They could also be spoken by another person who has rehearsed with the storyteller.

The Temptation of Jesus in the Wilderness

Today our story is about how Jesus was tempted by Satan in the wilderness. Do you all know what "tempted" means? (*Wait for answers.*) That's right; it's like when someone asks you to do something that you know you're not supposed to do. Have any of you ever been tempted to do something that you know you shouldn't? (*Time for children to relate their stories.*) Those were all good examples of how we are tempted to do something that we know is wrong. In our story for today Jesus finds himself in a tough spot. He is being tempted and tested at the same time. Let's see how

Jesus faces temptation and passes his test with a perfect score.

Jesus was led into the wilderness by the Spirit so that he could be tempted and tested by the devil (*point to first picture*). You can imagine how scary it would be for you or me to spend even one night alone in a strange wilderness with nobody to talk to us. But Jesus didn't just stay one night out there alone; he stayed 40 days and 40 nights in the wilderness (*point to picture of 40 days and nights*). Jesus got hungry by day and cold by night. For 40 days and nights—just like Noah on the ark—Jesus prayed (*fold your hands*) and thought about what was to come. Finally the tempter came to Jesus. He knew that Jesus was pretty tired and hungry. This was the best time to try to get Jesus to slip up. (*In a mocking voice:*) "Now's the time to strike!" the devil thought. "Now that he's feeling tired and hungry and out of sorts, it will be easy to trip him up."

So the devil said (*hold up stone props*), "If you're the Son of God, tell these stones to become bread." Now you and I would have said, "Okay, I'm so hungry I'll turn them into bread" (*point to bread prop*). But Jesus said to the devil, "Man doesn't live by bread alone, but on every word that comes from the mouth of God." So Jesus withstood the first temptation. He passed the test that you and I would have failed.

Then the devil took Jesus to the top of the temple (*point to picture*) and said, "If you're the Son of God, throw yourself down." Then he thought that he could fool Jesus with some words from the Scriptures. He said, "Scriptures say that God will send angels (*point to picture of angels*) to protect you and lift you up in their hands (*make holding gesture with hands*) so that you won't hit your foot on a stone (*point to stone prop*). But Jesus said, "It is also written: 'Do not put the Lord your God to the test.' "

Now the devil was getting desperate. Jesus had passed both tests—Jesus—2, Satan—0! So the devil took Jesus up to a high mountain (*point to picture of mountain*) and showed him the whole world (*point all around the room*). He told Jesus of the riches of all the kingdoms of the world. He pointed out how beautiful they were and how comfortable Jesus would be and how much Jesus would have, if only he would bow down and worship at the devil's feet. But Jesus said (*gesture with a "push away" and a shout*), "Away from me, Satan! For it is written, 'Worship the Lord your God, and serve him only.' "

When the devil heard Jesus say these words, he knew that he had lost. Jesus had remained faithful. He had passed the tests. Then angels (*point to picture of angels*) came to attend to Jesus.

As you can see, the 11-verse story that appears in Matthew 4 has been enlarged considerably. There is an introduction in which the words *tempted* and *tested* are discussed and in which the children are given a chance to ask questions and to relate their own experiences to the class before the actual story is told. Techniques like these help to establish a foundation on which the storyteller can build. They define ideas and vocabulary that children may be unfamiliar with and they set the stage for the telling. All too often, we fail to set the stage and, as a result, children are not ready to receive the story. Getting children ready to listen and having them understand the basic vocabulary of the story will enable you to teach the meaning of the story more effectively.

If you outline the story, use props and pictures, and have a mental picture of the plot, you will be able to tell stories trippingly off the tongue. Practice these techniques until they become second nature, and don't worry if you make a mistake. It is inevitable that you will make one sometime during the course of your storytelling. Somewhere, sometime, you will forget a line, skip an episode, or get your tongue tied as you tell the story. Teachers can be such perfectionists that when they make a mistake they think that it's the end of the world (or at least the end of the lesson). Teachers and storytellers always travel light: When something goes wrong, they don't let it bother them; they keep on going. Don't let minor lapses of memory ruin your day. Children will understand if something goes wrong or if you forget your place in the story. It is important for you to remember to let little mistakes go. Don't let them ruin the lesson for you or your students.

Story Reading

How to Read Stories to Children

Practice … Practice … Practice … If you're going to read stories to children, you will have to take the time to practice reading aloud. One of the subjects I teach is Children's Literature, so I get lots of practice reading stories to my college students and to the children in the college's day care center. Reading to my three children also helped me to develop my oral reading skills.

> *Note: My three boys taught me to never skip over anything in the story. Children want the whole story. If you try to skip a few parts (because you're tired and want to stop reading so you can get to sleep), they will make it clear that skipping over parts of the story is a very bad reading practice.*

I am a better reader today than I was 20 years ago. The reason why is that I have given myself permission to practice by reading out loud—and often. Here are some techniques that I've found effective in reading stories aloud:

1. Choose stories to read aloud that *you* enjoy.

It's hard to be an enthusiastic reader if you really don't like the story that you're reading. If you choose stories that you personally enjoy, you will have a much better chance of being a successful reader.

2. Read slowly.

When you read to your students, make sure that you read slowly—especially when reading to younger children. Reading slowly does not mean that you drag the story out or that you read so slowly that you put the children to sleep. Rather, read at a pace that allows you not only to articulate the words but to add vocal expression as well. Children will respond better if they have some time to think about what you are reading.

3. Use your voice to create different characters.

Reading at a reasonable pace will allow you to add vocal interest to the story. You can, for example, change your voice to fit the personality of the characters of the story. You can also add sound effects where they are called for (e.g., the sound of "a mighty rushing wind"; stamp your feet for marching; imitate a lion's roar in the Daniel story; add other swooshes, bangs,

crashes, and crunches to enliven the story). If you are reading too fast, you will not have time to add vocal interest. Practice using different voices for your characters so that they will come alive as you read.

4. Use your face.

Because your hands are busy holding the book, your head becomes a most important tool for expression. Knitting your brows, opening your eyes wide, shaking or nodding your head, and using other facial expressions will help your audience interpret what is happening in the story.

5. Read phrases, not individual words.

If you have practiced your reading enough, you will be able to read phrases instead of individual words. By reading phrases you will be able to look at your audience and communicate your facial and vocal expressions with greater ease. Practice keeping one eye on the page and one eye on your audience. When you see the reactions of your audience to the reading, you will have a better idea of how to pace and express what you are reading.

6. Respond positively to questions and comments.

It is not unusual for readers to be interrupted with questions or comments from children. Sometimes readers become frustrated with children when they interrupt the flow of the reading. It is important to respond to questions and comments that children have and not become flustered when they voice their opinion or ask a question during the course of the reading. Remember that questions are important to children (especially younger children) and that answering them is a big part of teaching. It is always a good idea to anticipate questions that children may have and try to address them in a short introduction to the story. Explain where and when the story takes place, describe the characters, and discuss unfamiliar words with the children before you start reading the story.

7. Listen to yourself read aloud.

Use an audiocassette tape recorder to tape yourself as you read aloud. When you play it back, you will get a better feel for how you read and how you might improve your reading pace and expression. A videotape recording is even better for evaluating your performance. It also allows you to see how your audience is reacting.

8. Use your public library.

The public library is one of the richest sources of material for teaching the faith. The children's book section of the library is filled with books that deal with topics that relate to the lives of children, and hence their faith-life as well. In addition, the religion sections of your library will provide you with many excellent books that retell and illustrate the great stories of the Bible. The librarian in charge of the children's book section can help you in selecting and locating items that relate to the study of the Bible. You will also find that many libraries have extensive video-and audiocassette collections; some may be valuable to you in your study and teaching. Some public libraries also have video recording equipment, slide projectors, tape recorders, and other audiovisual aids you can check out.

In order to take advantage of the library resources, you will have to spend a little time finding out what kinds of resources your library has. Usually, libraries contain much more material than first meets the eye. Our tendency is to give up too quickly when trying to find materials. That's why

it's essential to set aside several hours to become familiar with the materials in the local library. I suggest that you (and/or your whole staff) even set up a meeting with the librarian to discuss what kinds of materials are available.

Librarians will also order specific items or search for them through inter-library loans. If you find something you need, you will probably be able to order it through your librarian. Make sure that you ask your librarian to show you some of the reference tools available for finding books on various subjects and topics.

Here are some reference tools that you might use to find books that deal with subjects of interest to teachers of the faith.

Best Books for Children

The Bookfinder

Bulletin of the Center for Children's Books

Booklinks

Children's Books in Print

Reading Picture Books

Picture books are sometimes defined as books in which the pictures can tell the story without using the text. There are also wordless picture books and books with only a few illustrations that enhance the text. Whatever definition you use, picture/illustrated books are very powerful resources for teaching the faith.

It is possible for you to "read" a picture book without using the exact words of the book. You can simply retell the story while showing the pictures, or have the children help you tell the story. (See reference list.)

Storytelling through Gospeldramas

I've coined the term *Gospeldrama* to refer to dramatic presentations of the Gospel lessons for the Sundays of the church year. Of course, some Gospel lessons are more easily dramatized than others.

If your church uses a preselected series of lessons for every Sunday of the year as well as other holy days, it's a good idea to preview each lesson in advance to see which one(s) you will want to dramatize. This may seem like a big job, but if you divide up the lessons among your staff, they can quickly report on the lessons that they feel are most suitable for Gospeldramatization. (What a mouthful!)

Gospeldramas are suitable for performance by a wide range of grade levels, but are usually performed best by children grades 5 through 12 and by adults. Gospeldramas can be performed with a minimum of rehearsal (scripts in hand) or may be highly rehearsed and memorized.

There are numerous ways to write and perform Gospeldramas. My Gospeldramas use a narrator(s) and characters. The narrator format is helpful because it allows one person to hold the drama together for the rest of the cast. The narrator can help to guide the pace of the action and prompt the cast if they forget where they are. Since rehearsal time for most of the dramas you do in class or for church is short, a narrator format also helps cut down on the amount of memorization required by a cast.

What follows is an example of a narration Gospeldrama. In this particular format, actors could be used to speak the various parts, or the narrator could direct the play as he or she reads the story while the actors pantomime the parts. This particular printing of the Gospeldrama includes references to almost all of the stage directions and props used. If you were giving this performance, you may or may not wish to use all the directions.

Following the drama, I have included tips on preparing for and directing Gospeldramas.

The Wasteful Son: A Story Retold and Dramatized from Luke 15:11–31

Introduction

(Narrator or other leader should define the following words before the play starts: inheritance, estate, famine, and wasteful. For example: "Sometimes this story is called the 'Prodigal Son.' Since 'prodigal' means 'wasteful,' our play is about a young man who ....")

Narrator: Once upon a time there was a very wealthy man who had two sons. (*Wealthy man and two sons appear.*)

Narrator: It so happened that one day the wealthy man's (*younger son comes forward*) younger son came to his father and demanded his inheritance.

Younger Son (*says or acts out in pantomime as narrator reads*): I want my share of your estate. I don't want to wait until you die before I can start enjoying my life.

Narrator: ... he said. His father was greatly saddened (*father bows head and cries in sadness*) by his son's words, but he agreed to divide this wealth between his two sons. (*Both sons come forward and receive a dollar in change from the father.*) After a few days the younger son packed up his belongings (*pantomime packing, or use a suitcase and pack some clothes, a teddy bear, and a few other "essentials"*) and took a trip to a far-off land. (*Here a number of things could be done: mime riding a horse, getting a taxi cab with driver asking where younger son wants to go, and/or riding a bus with people who will later take his money.*) There he spent his money as if he thought it would never run out. He spent his money on foolish things. (*Spends money on a new shirt; new athletic shoes; buys his girlfriend a diamond; etc.*) To become popular he threw many a party (*have a party with several other characters— mime, laugh, listen to recording of wild music, whatever looks partyish*) and wasted his money on loose living of all sorts. It was to this younger son's great dismay that about the time his money ran out a great famine swept over the land. (*Have someone sweep across the stage with a broom—a sign can hang around his/her neck saying "Great Famine," while other cast members start to moan and wail with appropriate "Ooooooooh's" and "Uggggggggh's."*) With his money all gone (*show empty pockets*) and food harder to find than a word in the dictionary that you don't know how to spell, the young boy began to get very hungry (*younger son rubs tummy and groans in hunger*). His stomach was soon as empty as his wallet; and so the starving young man

went to a local farmer and begged to be hired as a pig feeder. (*Farmer comes out with slop bucket and points to puppet pigs [or cast members dressed as pigs] at side of stage. The boy feeds pigs as they eat out of the bucket.*) The boy became so hungry that the pig food started to look very good to him. (*Boy licks lips and tries to get at the slop, but pigs push him away.*)

Younger Son: Even the pigs are fed better than I am. (*Pigs nod yes with enthusiasm.*)

Narrator: … he thought.

Young Son: And still no one will give me anything to eat. (*Pigs nod no slowly and sadly.*)

Narrator: After much suffering, the lad finally came to his senses. (*A booing sound effect from the pigs*). He said to himself,

Young Son: At home even my father's hired hands have more to eat than I do. (*Hired hands at side of stage can pantomime eating lots of good things; yum—yum sounds.*) I'm dying of hunger, and they have food to spare! (*Hired hands say "pass the potatoes, pass the corn, pass the peas, pass the butter," and other words to that effect.*) I will go home to my Father and say: Father, I have sinned against God and against you, I'm not even worthy to be called your son. Please take me on as a hired hand.

Narrator: This he resolved to do. And so it was that he journeyed home to his father. (*Younger son starts to pantomime walking.*)

Narrator: While he was still quite a way from home, his father saw him in the distance (*father makes binoculars with his hands and spots his son*) and was filled with pity (*mime pity*) and love (*hands on heart*) for his son. He ran as fast as his old feet could carry him. (*Father and younger son pantomime "slow motion run" as they come together. The theme from "Chariots of Fire" can be played or hummed in the background.*) And when he reached his son, he threw his arms around him (*they embrace with lots of back slapping and hugs*) and kissed him. (*Kissing is always difficult for kids, so just do it the best you can—or not at all. I suggest that the father take the son's head in his hands and kiss the top of his head.*) The young boy said,

Young Son (*on his knees with head bowed*): Father, I have sinned against both God and you, and I am not worthy to be called your son.

Narrator: But before his son could say another word, his father called to his servants and said,

Father: Bring the finest robes in the house and put them on him. (*Servants appear and run to get robes and jewels and shoes—the more outlandish the jewelry, the better.*) And bring a jeweled ring for his finger and a new pair of shoes! And kill the calf that we have in the fattening pen. (*Servants bring out cardboard cut-out of fat calf on platter.*) We are going to have the biggest celebration of our lives. (*Servants all yell yeah!*) Prepare the feast, for this son of mine was dead and now is alive again; he was lost, but now he is found!

Narrator: And so the party began. (*Blow noise makers and throw confetti in the air. The cast then freezes in place while the narrator continues.*) Now, in the meantime, the older son was out in the fields at work. (*Older son appears with rake in hand and pantomimes work.*) As he returned home (*older son starts toward "frozen party"*), he heard the sounds of music and dancing coming from the house. (*Party people unfreeze and party on, singing and dancing.*) He asked one of the servants what was going on, and the servant replied,

Servant (*moving toward older son*): Your brother has come home, and your father has killed the fattest calf (*partygoers hold up calf and point to it in a "Price Is Right" technique*) and prepared a great feast (*everyone eats heartily*) to celebrate his safe return home!

Narrator: The older brother angrily said to his father,

Older Brother (*speaking to his father*): All these years I've worked very hard for you (*holds up rake and shakes it*) and never once have I disobeyed you. (*All eyes of all partygoers are on the older son—especially the eyes of young son, who looks on in shame.*) In all that time you never gave me even one young goat so that I could have a feast with my friends. Yet when this son (*pointing to younger son in disgust*) of yours comes back after wasting your money, you kill the finest calf and celebrate with a party.

Narrator: The old man held his son and said,

Father (*arm around older son*): My dear son, you and I are very close, and all that is mine is yours. But, listen to me (*points finger at ear*). It's right to celebrate (*all partygoers throw confetti and blow party horns; then they freeze in position again*). For he is your brother (*younger son comes to father— father places arm around him also*), and he was dead and has come back to life! He was lost, but now he is found! (*All partygoers celebrate with confetti and horns again briefly.*)

Optional: Singing "Amazing Grace! How Sweet the Sound" (*LW* 509)

Stanza 1: Younger Son (solo, or in pantomime as congregation sings)

> Amazing Grace! How sweet the sound
> That saved a wretch like me!
> I once was lost but now am found,
> Was blind but now I see!

Stanza 2: Older son may sing

> The Lord has promised good to me,
> His word my hope secures;
> He will my shield and portion be
> As long as life endures.

Stanza 3: Younger son may sing

> Through many dangers, toils, and snares
> I have already come;
> His grace has brought me safe so far,
> His grace will see me home.

All may sing stanza 4 in two- or three-part canon (round).

> Yes, when this flesh and heart shall fail
> And mortal life shall cease,
> Amazing grace shall then prevail
> In heaven's joy and peace.

Whole Cast: *All praise to the Father* (point up). *All praise to the Son* (point from sky to ground). *All praise to the Spirit* (point from side to side, making sign of the cross)—*three* (point to sky with three fingers) *in one* (index finger points to sky).

Tips on Directing Gospeldramas

General Considerations

Even if you have authored the script, you will probably have to read it several times to make sure that you have everything straight. When I've gone over the script several times, I think of new ways to help children interpret the dialog. When you go over the play, make sure that you write down all the things that you want to add in the margin or on a separate sheet of paper. Use the line numbers as reference points as you make your notes. Let's walk through the script and see what needs to be done as we get ready to direct.

1. Look at and think about everything in the script, no matter how insignificant it may seem at first. For example, if you are basing the Gospeldrama on a parable, what's a parable? Will the cast know who told the story? Have they read the account in the Bible beforehand? Do they know what all the words mean? Do they have a sense of the location and what it was like?

2. Follow any implicit directions in the Bible account. Almost every story has implicit directions built right in—a person does here or there, does this or that, looks sad or happy, etc. With a little practice and imagination (and a willingness to risk), you will be able to dramatize almost any story.

3. Who will be in the cast? Just your class? Anyone from the high school department? How many students do you need to fill the roles? If you don't have enough students, can you and another teacher, the pastor, or some other adult improvise as fill-ins?

If you have more students than parts in the script, consider using several narrators. Many times, that's a plus. Several narrators can add vocal variety to the performance as well as take pressure off just one. Besides, many children would rather share the "burden of stardom" than stand alone. (Stage fright is very real to some people. Be sensitive and encouraging at all times.) Use your good judgment—you know your children better than anyone else.

Take a look at the cast list in the script and decide how you will select the cast. Sometimes volunteers will come to the fore, and at other times you may wish to ask students to play different parts. Depending on how sophisticated you want to get, you may even have tryouts. For most purposes, however, a competitive tryout is unnecessary and undesirable. Try to maximize student participation; get as many children involved in different aspects of the play as you can.

Here is where it's very important to know your students. As you do other Gospeldramas during the year, you will be able to involve more students in a variety of roles (lead parts, crew, sound effects, song leaders, bit parts, etc.). Remember: This is a team effort to help people understand the Gospel; it's not a competition.

4. Consider using cue cards for audience and actors. Cue cards, if not overly used, can help shorten rehearsal time and make one-time performances go just a bit more smoothly.

Sometimes you may wish to use cue cards for the audience so they too can become part of the action. The audience could be encouraged to add sound effects ("swoosh" as famine sweeps the land, "ooooooh" to sympathize with a character, "murmur" for the crowds, etc). Cue cards for the audience can add to the festive feeling of the drama and help to keep the actors on track. Cue- card holders also become important members of the cast (especially if not everyone can have a speaking part). Get as many of the students involved in the play as you can.

5. As you read each line and any stage direction, try to imagine what the play will look and sound like. That's hard to do. Plays by their very nature are meant to be performed live. When you read them silently, you need to use lots of imagination to see and hear the play in the theater of your mind. However hard it is, drawing a mental picture is an important part of your preparation for the play. The more you familiarize yourself with the play, the more you will be able to envision how it will be played out with *your* cast and in *your* facilities.

6. Plan to use simple props, scenery, costumes, and, if necessary, puppets. Simple props such as hats, cardboard or projected scenery, and puppets can add variety to any performance.

Decide if you want to play this in a French accent with beret or just play it straight. (See note in prop list on page 71.) But don't try to do something that your cast is not capable of. Don't do the French accent thing if nobody can do a French accent. Always remember that suggestions made in the script are just suggestions—not hard and fast rules.

It is not necessary to work for hours and hours to produce scenery. Keep it as simple as possible. Children will enjoy making or painting scenery, wearing costumes, and acting as puppeteers (more on puppets in the next chapter). In this way you will maximize participation for both the cast and crew.

7. Use music and other special effects whenever you can. Look for appropriate places in the Gospeldrama. The music doesn't have to be elaborate; it may only be some humming in the background, the playing of a pre-recorded tape, or the singing of a snippet of a familiar song. Whenever you use music, you add excitement to a performance.

In addition, using music and special effects gives members of the crew a chance to participate in the action of the play. They also provide an outlet for creativity and contribute to the dramatic telling of the story.

8. Determine any staging you may need. Many Gospeldramas require no particular form of stage setup. That doesn't mean you can't set up something more elaborate. Time and budget constraints will always have some effect on staging. In general it's best to keep staging simple, but if you

have lighting and/or other staging resources, go ahead and use what you have.

9. Consider asking the cast to memorize their parts. Having children memorize their lines is a good practice. Parents can become involved in the play with their children as they help them learn their lines. (My sons, David and Andrew, and I once performed in a play together. We helped each other memorize our lines and practiced them at home and in the car as we went to rehearsals. This was good modeling for my children because they saw that Dad had to struggle through learning his lines just as they did.) Plus, when parents participate this way, they look forward to seeing the play all the more.

10. Plan your rehearsal(s). The number of rehearsals you have will depend on the length and complexity of your play. For most Gospeldramas, you will probably not need to schedule more than one or two rehearsals. The rehearsal for one Gospeldrama I directed was rehearsed this way:

On Saturday evening we spent about an hour and a half reading through the script and blocking the action. We ran through the play about four times. The first time took about 40 minutes; the second about 25; the third about 15; and the last about 12 minutes.

Sunday morning the entire cast met before church and quickly ran through the play. I gave them some last minute directions and we were ready to go.

How much time should you allow for practice? Sometimes you can accomplish just as much in a short amount of time as you can with lots and lots of rehearsal. There is a delicate balance between rushing into the performance without adequate rehearsal and over rehearsing. If you need a little more time to polish what you are doing, take it; but don't spend five hours of rehearsal for a five-minute play. If you are spending too much time in rehearsal, you probably need to look at how thoroughly you have prepared.

Before Practice Begins

1. Block your performance. "Blocking" means telling people where to stand, sit, run, and otherwise move on the stage. To block the play, read the script carefully and make notes in the margin to remind yourself where you want the children to move, sit, and stand.

Even though the definition sounds simple, it is difficult to block a performance. If you have ever directed 75 children in a Christmas Eve service, you know that getting them to stand, sit, and turn around at the same time is no easy job. This is why you need to take some time to figure out where you want the children to enter and exit, stand and sit, run and walk, move or freeze in their tracks. It will take time to figure out what you want them to do and when; but whatever you do, do it before the rehearsal. There is no right or wrong way to block a play; mostly it takes common sense and experimentation

Prepared or purchased scripts sometimes give detailed stage directions, but more often than not you will have to modify and create your own blocking because your "stage" will have its own unique characteristics.

2. Make sure you have all the props ready to use when you get to rehearsal.

Look over the prop list and make sure you have all the things you need when you start to rehearse. Since most Gospeldramas are done with a minimum of rehearsal, you need to make each run-through as real as you can.

3. Get all special effects ready before you start. Special effects, music, and other extras should also be ready to go as the rehearsal starts. It's very important to rehearse *with* the effects. You will probably find that it takes a little extra time to rehearse with the effects, but if you don't rehearse them during the rehearsal, you will never work out the bugs. If your special-effects crew can rehearse by themselves before you get everyone together, you will probably have a smoother dress rehearsal.

Tips for During Practice

1. Feel free to risk trying something different. Remember that you can always change an idea if you find that it doesn't work out dramatically. Every situation is different; what might be suitable for one situation may not work in another. Be flexible, and don't be afraid to try out ideas you have or ideas that the cast may suggest as you go about your rehearsal. I've found that the cast usually will come up with the most exciting ideas if they are encouraged to make suggestions.

2. Read through the script around a table before you walk through it. Children need to hear the words before they "do" the words. Get into a circle and read the script (along with the stage directions) with the children.

Depending on the age of the children and the complexity of the play, your reading may be highly directed or informal. In any case, you should take time to read through the script so that everyone has an idea of what the play is about.

Reading the play also affords you the opportunity to discuss its meaning right from the start. Stop to explain the meaning of lines whenever you think clarification is necessary. Once everyone understands the play, you'll be ready to start putting all the pieces of the play together.

2b. As you read the play—interpret it. The most important thing you are doing is telling the Bible story. If you forget the meaning of the play, if you forget that you are teaching the faith through this dramatic experience, you are missing the point. You must take the time to comment on the meaning of the play, to interpret the story for the children.

When you read through the drama, the actors have an opportunity to think about what is happening in the story. They can ask questions, comment on the action, think about why Jesus told the story, and become actively involved with the story. As a teacher of the faith, you can use the dramatic format to instruct and interpret the story for and with the children.

And you can do something else. As you rehearse, instruct, and interpret the story, you will also teach children how to respect, help, and support each other as they praise God with their words and actions. Telling the story is an act of praise. Acting the story out is another way in which we can proclaim the messages of God to all people.

As you rehearse, you will have the opportunity to teach more than just the script. You will be teaching children all sorts of things about the life, faith, trust, friendship, and joy that comes from praising God together. We

"do" the drama in praise to God; not as a praise to ourselves. This is not to say that we can't rejoice in a performance well done. Joy is also a gift of God.

As we work on any performance (from a lowly puppet play to a full-blown three act musical extravaganza), we are celebrating the gifts that God has given to us. When we proclaim the Gospel, celebrate it, and share our gifts with one another in faith, we give glory to God. We can do that every time we dramatically tell the great stories of the Bible.

3. Don't worry if every line isn't perfect. If a child doesn't say the line exactly as written, don't get too upset about it. Minor deviations from the script are bound to happen (even in professional theater). If your actor gets the main idea of the line across, rejoice in spite of the imperfection. Better to get the gist of the line across than to say no line at all.

4. Block the drama with the actors. If possible, have the children write the blocking movements in their scripts so they will have a mental picture of what they are supposed to do. Then walk through the script with the children as they read or say their lines from memory. (Here's where memorization of lines will be of great help—your cast won't have to rely on the script and can pay attention to what they are doing.)

Blocking with the cast is really lots of fun and will actually help the children remember what they are supposed to do. If you break the play down into smaller episodes (just like when you try to remember episodes for storytelling) and rehearse each in sequence, you will find that the children will quickly learn and that they more easily remember what to do and say.

5. Practice speaking toward the audience. Try to make sure your actors have their faces turned toward the audience as much as possible when they speak their lines. This takes some practice because it sometimes feels unnatural. In normal conversation we usually look directly at each other. On a stage, however, we are talking not only to the actors on stage, but to the audience as well.

6. Projecting the voice. In addition to speaking toward the audience, your cast must practice vocal projection. However, there is a great difference between shouting the lines and speaking in a voice that projects to the audience. Shouting is not the answer; it only hurts the voice. Help children project by using all their vocal mechanism. Encourage them to stand straight and use good posture, keep their lungs filled with air, open their mouths, and articulate each word. Encourage them to speak in such a way that their voices can be heard at a distance without straining with a shout or scream. For that you need to warm up.

7. Warm-ups (getting rid of the butterflies). Whether you are performing a play, leading an echo pantomime, or teaching a lesson, it is important to warm up before you start. Warming up not only helps you avoid voice strain, it also helps you get rid of the butterflies. Here are a series of exercises that will help you warm up for a play or, for that matter, your first class session.

a. Roll your shoulders slowly around and up to your neck. If you are with a friend, give each other a shoulder rub.

b. Put the palms of your hands together in front of you and push them

together for five seconds. Relax. Repeat three or four times.

c. Stand straight, with feet about a shoulder apart. Tighten all the muscles of your body for a few seconds, then relax. Repeat three times.

d. Clench your fists in front of you while curling your arms up to your chest. Breathe in and out slowly as you curl your arms.

e. Stand on your toes and reach for the sky at the same time. Repeat several times.

f. Take a slow, deep breath, then let it all out slowly. Relax for a moment and repeat. Relax and repeat once more. (Warning: Do not do deep breathing too fast; it could cause you to feel light-headed.)

g. Take another deep breath, clench your teeth, and hiss it out through your teeth. Repeat once more, making sure that you expel as much air as you can. Relax for a moment.

h. Put your hand on the top of your head. Take a deep breath and hummmmmmmm (emphasis on the mmmmmm's) so that you can feel the vibrations of the hum through the top of your head and into your hand. Repeat three times.

i. Pretend that you are chewing a piece of taffy. Make your jaw work up and down, side to side. Move your tongue around your mouth as if you are trying to loosen a piece of taffy stuck on your teeth. Do this for about 30 seconds.

j. Yawn several times while gently massaging your jaw muscles.

k. Put your hand on your tummy, just above your belly-button. In rapid succession say "Haaa, haaa, haaa, haaa, haaa" (that's five haaa's). Your hand should push in every time you say "Haaa." If your hand goes out on each haaa, you are breathing incorrectly.

l. With your mouth wide open, say "Aaaah." Now start with a low-tone aaaah and slide your voice to a high pitched aaaah and back down again. Repeat several times.

Several things will happen to you when you do these exercises: 1) You should feel better than you did when you started, because you have been doing some mild exercises that cause you to breathe with a little more intensity than you normally do; 2) your voice should now be warmed up so that you are less likely to strain it; and 3) because your blood is flowing a bit more, you will be less prone to the butterflies.

Exercises like these can help to calm a case of the jitters for both children and adults. If you're nervous about making a presentation or if you're about to lead the children in an echo pantomime, it is good practice to do some warm-ups beforehand. Take a few moments to do some warm-ups with your children before they perform a play, read, or speak in front of a group.

Warm-ups are also useful if you notice that your class is getting a little sleepy or not paying attention. If this happens, take a few moments to stretch, hum, and roll the shoulders. The class will feel better and be more receptive to the lesson.

8. Practice "jumping" on the lines. Pauses between lines make everyone nervous. Encourage the cast to "jump" on lines after they are delivered. That is, actors must anticipate the next line and immediately speak it without hesitation. Whether actors have memorized the script or are reading from it, they must not hesitate when it is their turn to say a line.

How to Use a More Conventional Script

The following conventional script is based on the parable of "The Workers in the Vineyard." It has more explicit stage directions, prop list, cast list, and other suggestions for performance. Before you read the script, spend a little time studying Matthew 20:1–16.

Reading the original story always helps you to understand the dramatization better. Before you give your cast the script, read through the original story with them as well. Then, as you read through the script, have each member of the cast underline or highlight his or her individual lines. Have members of the crew highlight any props or special effects materials that they need and make note of where any sound effects or lighting cues are located. No matter how small their part or how simple their special effect, everybody is important to the play.

As you read "The Parable of the Workers in the Vineyard" try to envision the drama as performed in the space you have to work with and begin thinking of how you might script a Gospeldrama for your class.

The Parable of the Workers in the Vineyard: A Gospeldrama based on Matthew 20:1–16

The Cast: (*any part may be played by men or women, girls or boys*)

Narrator

A Landowner

A Foreman

The Time Clock (rooster crow and whistle. "Time")

First Laborer(s) at 6:00 a.m. ("L1")

Second Laborer(s) at 9:00 a.m. ("L2")

Third Laborer(s) at noon ("L3")

Fourth Laborer(s) at 3:00 p.m. ("L4")

Last Laborer(s) at 5:00 p.m. ("L5")

Note: The parts of the Foreman and the Timeclock can be played by the same person. If one has a very small cast, the Laborers can be rotated out to substitute for the other laborers.

Props: Five index cards (3″ × 5″) used as time cards; one beret for the landowner (if played with a French accent as a Frenchman/woman); five fake denarius bills; four "Unfair Signs" stating: a) "Management Unfair to Labor"; b) "Equal Pay for Equal Work"; c) "On Strike"; d) "Laborers Unite"; Extra costumes, hats, etc., are optional at the director's discretion.

Sound Effects: 1) Large boom box to play recordings; 2) Excerpt recording (on audiocassette tape) of the William Tell Overture "wake up" music—flute solo from William Tell, often heard in Bugs Bunny cartoons; 3) Excerpt recording (on audiocassette tape) of Tennessee Ernie Ford's "Sixteen Tons": "You load sixteen tons, what do you get? Another day older and deeper in debt. Saint Peter, don't you call me 'cause I can't go!" (cut off at that point).

Staging: Any form of stage can be used: in the round at center of congregation, in or in front of the chancel area, or on conventional stage. Lighting is not important. If lights can be raised as "day begins" without difficulty, it is appropriate to do so. Stage directions are given in parentheses.

Note: It is very important that the action be lively, exaggerated, and crisp. It is also very important for cast members to jump on their lines. Pausing too long between lines will slow the pace of the action and cause the audience to wander. Before starting to rehearse on stage, it is wise to read through the entire play to get a feeling of what each cast member is expected to do. Underlining or highlighting lines, cue lines, and other important bits of business is also a good practice.

The Parable of the Workers in the Vineyard

(The Gospel lesson is announced by the narrator as the actors take their places upstage: a line facing the audience.)

1. **Narrator:** The Gospel for today is taken from the 20th chapter of St. Matthew, starting with the first verse.

2. **Narrator and cast say together:** The Parable of the Workers in the Vineyard,

3. **Narrator** (*taking place at center stage*): or—The First Shall Be Last, and the Last Shall Be First. (*Pause while Landowner takes place on center stage in front of the Narrator and pretends to be asleep.*)

4. **Narrator:** The kingdom of heaven is like a landowner who got up early in the morning .... (*Music cue: William Tell Overture played softly as wake-up music.*)

5. **Time Clock:** (*As music begins, Time Clock does rooster crow.*) Cock-a-doodle-doooo! (*The landowner wakes with a stretch to the rooster crow.*)

6. **Narrator:** ... and went out to hire men to work in his vineyard.

7. **Landowner:** I'll give you one denarius for a day's work.

8. **L1:** It's a deal! (*They shake hands. L1 goes to the Time Clock, who hands him/her a card. L1 pulls down the hand of the Time Clock, who bites on the card with a ka-chunk sound, imitating a punch clock.*)

9. **Time Clock** (*in a mechanical voice*): Worker in—6 a.m.

10. **L1:** (*Pantomimes work: picks grapes, puts them in basket, puts basket*

in truck, wipes brow—repeating in a set rhythm as the drama continues.)

11. **Narrator:** The landowner went to the marketplace at 9 o'clock and saw others who were doing nothing. He told them ...

12. **Landowner** (*to L2*): You also go and work in my vineyard, and I'll pay you what is right. (*L2 goes to Time Clock and repeats actions by L1.*)

13. **Time Clock:** Worker in—9 o'clock a.m.

14. **Narrator:** And the landowner went out at noon.

15. **Landowner** (*to L3*): You also go into my vineyard, and I'll pay you what is right. (*L3 repeats Time Clock actions and works in rhythm with other laborers.*)

16. **L3:** Worker in—12 noon.

17. **Narrator:** And the landowner did the same at 3 o'clock.

18. **Landowner:** Get to work—I'll pay you what's right! (*L4 repeats stage business.*)

19. **Time Clock:** Worker in—3 o'clock p.m.

20. **Narrator:** Now about 5 o'clock in the afternoon the Landowner went out and found still others (*or "another" if cast is small*) standing around. And he asked them [him/her],

21. **Landowner:** Why have you been standing here all day long doing nothing?

22. **L5:** Because nobody has hired us [me]!

23. **Narrator:** So he said to them [him] ...

24. **Landowner:** You also go and work in my vineyard.

25. **Narrator:** And so the last laborer went to work in the landowner's vineyard very late in the day.

26. **Time Clock:** Worker in—5 p.m. (*L5 goes to Time Clock, punches in, and loads only one basket of grapes. As soon as he/she has wiped his/her brow, Time Clock blows a whistle.*)

27. **Time Clock:** Hoooooooooooo! Quitin' time! (*The laborers punch out on the Time Clock in turn, the last first and the first last. All laborers pantomime exhaustion, except the last laborer, who is still very fresh.*)

28. **Narrator:** Now the workers who were hired first expected to be paid more because they had worked longer. But when the Foreman handed out the pay, each received one denarius.

29. **Foreman:** (*Hands out a denarius to each laborer in turn. L1 through*

L4 notice that L5 is paid the same as they. They begin to grumble in silent stage voice.)

30. **Narrator:** And they began to grumble.

31. **L1–4** (*loudly*): Grumble, grumble, grumble!

32. **Narrator:** And they protested to the Landowner …

33. **L1:** These [This] men [man] who were [was] hired last worked only one hour!

34. **L2:** And you have made them [him] equal to us who have borne the heat of the day!

35. **L1–4** (*at random*): You're unfair! Unfair! Strike! Down with management! (*They pick up unfair/strike, etc., signs as the music to "Sixteen Tons" begins. They march in a circle around the Landowner as they sing along with the lyrics—or sing without the music.*) "You load sixteen tons. . . . Saint Peter, don't you call me 'cause I can't goooooooooo!" (*They hold note even after the music cuts out until the Landowner begins to speak.*)

36. **Landowner:** Hold on, cut, wait just … a … minute! (*Short pause as the laborers look at him in anticipation.*) Friend(s), I'm NOT being unfair to you.

37. **L1–4** (*looking at each other and then at the Landowner*): You're not?!

38. **Landowner:** No, I'm not. Didn't you agree to work for a denarius? (*They look at each other and then back to the Landowner and nod their heads yes twice in unison.*) Take your pay and go. I want to give the man who was hired last the same as I gave you. Don't I have the right to do what I want with my own money? (*The laborers look at each other and then to the Landowner and nod their heads three times quickly, in unison.*) Or are you envious because I am generous?

(*They look at each other and then down at their feet in shame and nod their heads four times quickly, in unison.*)

39. **Narrator:** And so it can be truly said …

40. **All Cast:** That the last will be first (*L5 stands tall),* and the first *(the first laborers sink to their knees)* shall be last! ALL PRAISE TO THE FATHER (*all point up with their right hands*), ALL PRAISE TO THE SON (*all point down with right hands*), ALL PRAISE TO THE SPIRIT (*all make the sign of the cross vertically*), THREE (*all hold up three fingers on right hand*) IN ONE! (*All point to the sky with index finger pointing up. All hold hands and take one bow, and exit.*)

One More Gospeldrama for You to Try

Here's one more Gospeldrama for you to try with your children. It's based on the story of "The Wise and Foolish Builders" (Matthew 7:24–27) and was performed by 9th–12th graders at a regional youth gathering. I rehearsed for two hours with a group of enthusiastic young people who had already memorized the main character's lines. Nothing is more fun than working with young people who are eager to share the Gospel and their gifts with their peers. Try this Gospeldrama the next time the story of "The Wise and Foolish Builders" is used as a lesson for the day, or as an "in house" play for your Sunday school or vacation Bible school classes. Whenever possible, give your older students a chance to proclaim the message to their younger counterparts. This is a great way to give older students an opportunity for service in the church.

The Parable of the Wise and Foolish Builders—Based on Matthew 7:24–27: A Gospeldrama

The Cast: Parts may be played by either men or women as they are available: Narrator, Wise Man, Foolish Man, Contractor, 16–18 Construction Workers (CW), who will take on various bit parts throughout the performance. Note: If there is a limited cast, the parts of the Narrator, Wise Man, Foolish Man, and Builder can be doubled up as needed.

Props: 1) Paper-mâché rock (approximately 5′w × 3′h × 3′w) painted gray; 2) One 6′ × 6′ piece of plastic (polyurethane) drop cloth (6 mil.); 3) Three or four buckets filled with clean sand; 4) Optional: a wheelbarrow (sand in wheelbarrow used for building house on sand); 5) Four sets of blueprints: a) house of straw, b) house of sticks, c) house of bricks, d) two cathedral drawings; 6) Assorted tools such as hammers, saws, tool belts, hard hats, rulers, pieces of lumber (short 2′ × 4′s), level, shovel; 7) One small bell; 8) One sign saying "ACME CONSTRUCTION COMPANY—WE BUILD ANYWHERE!" (approximately 4′ × 6′, white or yellow, with black lettering); 9) Confetti for snow; 10) Optional: an electric fan (to blow confetti snow); 11) Several camera flash attachments (for lightning affects); 12) Several squirt guns or bottles filled with water (for rain affect); 13) Two large blue cloth sheets (approx. 10′ × 2′) for water wave affect; 14) One cardboard cut-out television screen, 25″ diagonally, with words "WEATHER BULLETIN" written on top and bottom.

Sound Affects: 1) PA system with mike and cassette tape recorder inputs; 2) One cassette tape player; 3) Audiocassette tape(s) with recordings of: a) Wagner's "Flight of the Valkyries," b) "Storm Music" from the William Tell Overture, c) "Rock around the Clock," by Bill Halley and the Comets.

Staging: Any form of stage can be used—in the round, at center of the congregation, in or in front of the chancel area, or on a conventional stage. Lighting is not important, but if lights can be raised as drama begins, so much the better.

Note: It is very important that the action be lively, exaggerated, and crisp.

Cast members must jump on their lines. Pausing too long between lines or actions will slow the pace of the action and cause the audience to wander. Before rehearsal on stage, read through the entire play to get a feeling of what each cast member is expected to do. Underline or highlight lines, cue lines, and other important bits of business.

1. (*The Gospel lesson is announced by the Narrator as the actors take their places. They form a line(s) facing away from the audience.*)

2. **Narrator:** Our Lord and Savior told this parable. Listen to him for everyone who hears and puts these words into practice is like a wise man who built his house on ...

3. **Entire Cast** (*shouting as they turn and face the audience*): THE ROCK!

4. (*Cassette tape of "Rock around the Clock" is played as actors get into their places on the stage as follows:*

   a. One Construction Worker (CW) pretends to be a door; that is, he holds small bell in one hand. When Wise Man enters the office, CW rings bell.

   b. One or two CWs hold up sign: "ACME CONSTRUCTION COMPANY,—WE BUILD ANYWHERE!"

   c. Contractor looks with interest—nodding head, pointing to things on blueprints, etc.—at blueprints being shown by another CW.

   d. Other CWs stage talk about their work in pantomime.

   e. Wise Man enters—that is, he pantomimes his entrance through a door as CW rings bell to signal his entrance.)

5. **Construction Workers and Contractor** (*as bell rings, they say together*): A CUSTOMER!

   (*CWs quickly line up at attention. They hold tools in a formal frozen pose as Contractor inspects them as if they were soldiers at inspection. Meanwhile, the Wise Man reads the ACME CONSTRUCTION sign with great interest.*)

6. **Contractor:** Good morning! May I be of assistance?

7. **Wise Man:** Yes, I believe you can. Your advertisement says that you build anywhere.

8. **Contractor:** Yes indeed! That's our motto! Isn't that right, gang?

9. **CWs** (*in unison, with military precision and vigor*): YES SIR! ACME CONSTRUCTION—WE BUILD ANYWHERE!

10. **Wise Man:** Very impressive. Could you perhaps build a house for me on the rock?

11. **CWs** (*together*): ON THE ROCK! YES, SIR—ACME CONSTRUCTION—WE BUILD ANYWHERE!

12. **Contractor:** As you see, my crew and I are at your disposal. Exactly

what kind of house would you like to build?

13. **Wise Man:** I would like it to be the finest house that can be built.

14. **Contractor:** Say no more—allow me to show you some of our latest work. (*CWs bring out blueprint drawings as follows:*

   a. house of straw;

   b. house of sticks;

   c. house of bricks.

   At each of these the Wise Man shakes his head no and generally complains in stage voice and pantomime. At last a blueprint of a cathedral is brought out. The Wise Man responds happily.)

15. **Wise Man:** This is exactly what I was looking for. The perfect house to build on …

16. **Entire Cast:** THE ROCK!

17. **Narrator:** And so the Acme Construction Company began building a house for the Wise Man on the rock as they had been instructed.

   (*Workers bring rock on stage with pantomime actions. They serve as cranes to lift the rock; they jackhammer, shovel, pound on boards, saw lumber, etc. Eventually the CWs form a cathedral-like structure with their hands as they stand behind the rock.*)

18. **Narrator:** With every passing day the house began to take on shape, and in almost no time at all the house built on the rock was finished.

19. **Wise Man:** What a glorious house—and all of it built on …

20. **CWs** (*together as they look at the audience*): THE ROCK! (*CWs stamp one foot hard on the floor together after saying THE ROCK.*)

21. **Wise Man:** (*Enters the house and smiles.*)

22. **Narrator:** No sooner had the Wise Man taken up residence in his new home than he heard disturbing news.

   (*TV screen "WEATHER BULLETIN" is held in front of the Narrator. He continues in "Civil Defense Voice."*)

   This is your emergency channel. This is NOT a test; I repeat, this is NOT a test. A hurricanelike cyclocyclonic sub-tropical arctic air mass of unstable nature has been detected on Doppler 3-D radar and is moving in your direction. Take cover immediately!

   This is NOT a test; I repeat, this is NOT a test! If this had not been a test, your regularly scheduled programming would return after you heard a deafening beeeeeeep; but that's not going to happen because this is NOT a test!

   (*The TV screen is taken away, and the narrator continues … *)

And so ... (*Wagner Valkyrie music begins and increases in volume as the storm hits.*)

the rain came down (*squirt guns fired at house*)

and the streams rose (*blue cloths are made into waves that rise up and are shaken with greater intensity as the narration continues.*)

and the winds blew and beat against that house; (*confetti is thrown into the wind created by the cloth used for waves or by the electric fan. The actors doing the storm become less and less animated and eventually give up in exhaustion as music fades out.*)

yet it did not fall because it had its foundation on ...

23. **Entire Cast:** THE ROCK! (*All stamp once.*)

   (*"Rock around the Clock" is played again as the cast disassembles the house, picks up tools, set props back in position, and takes places as at start of the play at the Wise Man's entrance. Music fades.*)

24. **Narrator:** Ah, but human beings are of such a nature that even though they hear the words of our Lord and Master, they do not put them into practice. They are like the Foolish Man who built his house on sand. (*Here the same bits of business performed at the Wise Man's entrance are repeated.*)

25. **Foolish Man** (*entering door as bell rings. He speaks to the Contractor in a most haughty tone of voice.*): How do you do?

26. **Contractor:** Fine, thank you. Welcome to ACME CONSTRUCTION COMPANY ...

27. **CWs** (*together*): WE BUILD ANYWHERE!

28. **Foolish Man:** So I have heard. I would like to build a house. I have purchased some riverfront property that simply cries out for something grand, beautiful, expensive—in short, your best design.

   (*The Contractor shows him the cathedral blueprint.*)

   This is perfect. Now, can your company build this house on the beach by the river?

29. **CWs:** ON THE BEACH! YES SIR! ACME CONSTRUCTION COMPANY—WE BUILD ANYWHERE! (*Workers do much the same bits of business as they did for the House on the Rock. This time, however, they act as cranes and steam shovels, and they dump buckets of sand on the polyurethane drop cloths. They then build the same kind of cathedral-type house as before.*)

30. **Narrator:** So the house was completed, and it was a beautiful sight to behold.

31. **Foolish Man:** (*Steps into house and looks happy and satisfied with every-*

thing.) What a glorious house—and all of it built on ...

32. **CW's** (*together without a great deal of enthusiasm to the audience*): the sand.

33. **Narrator:** No sooner had the Foolish Man taken up residence in his new house than he heard disturbing news.

    (*Same bits of business as before: TV screen etc.*) This is your emergency channel. This is NOT a test; I repeat, this is NOT a test. A tornadolike anticyclonic multi-dimensional Canadian atmospheric disturbance of barometrically significant destructive power is headed in your direction. Take shelter in your house immediately. This is NOT a test! (*The TV screen is taken away.*)

    And so ... (*William Tell storm music comes up*) the rain came down, the streams rose, and the winds blew and beat against that house ... (*As this dialog continues, the house slowly starts to melt into the sand—the horror of the Foolish Man. The house stops melting about half way down.*)

    And it fell with a great crash!

34. **CWs** (*as they fall onto the Foolish Man and bury him in slow motion*): GREAAAAAT CRRRAAAASSSSSSSHHHHHHH!!!!!!

35. **Foolish Man** (*in small, squeaky voice*): Help! (*He expires with face in sand—the entire cast freezes in place.*)

36. **Narrator:** When Jesus had finished his story, the crowds were amazed at his teaching, because he taught as one who had authority, and not as their teachers of the law. (*The cast begins to slowly rise and form a line upstage.*)

    Therefore, it can be truly said that those who are wise build their foundation not on sand but on ...

37. **CWs:** THE ROCK ... (*They stamp once and point to the rock with their hands.*)

38. **Narrator:** ... who is Christ Jesus, our Lord.

39. **Entire Cast** (*holding hands and softly singing in unison stanza 1 of "My Hope Is Built on Nothing Less" [LW 368]*):

    My hope is built on nothing less
    Than Jesus' blood and righteousness;
    No merit of my own I claim
    But wholly lean on Jesus' name.
        On Christ, the solid rock, I stand;
        All other ground is sinking sand.

40. **Entire Cast:** All praise to the Father; (*They point with their right hand to the sky.*)

    All praise to the Son; (*They lower their hand and point to the ground.*)

All praise to the Spirit; (*They move their hand horizontally in the sign of the cross.*)

Three (*They hold up three fingers of their right hand*) in One! (*Point to the sky with index finger.*)

(*All turn and face the altar, bow their heads, divide, and exit off the sides of the stage.*)

The End.

As you can see, this Gospeldrama is a bit more complex than those that have come before. Each example that I have given you gets a bit more complex. Start off small with echo pantomimes and build to more complex dramatic presentations.

Remember to double up or split up parts when necessary. Also, don't be afraid to modify the cast parts and lines to fit your situation. For example: In the Gospeldrama of "The Wise and Foolish Builders," the narrator's part can be taken by two people, alternating. The narrator's "emergency bulletins" lines (lines 24 and 35) could easily be read by other announcers. In this way you can add a few more characters to the cast and shorten the narrator's memorization. As the leader, you have the freedom to double up and split up parts to suit your needs.

Don't feel you must always follow the script and directions *verbatim*. Take whatever liberties are necessary to do the best job with the maximum number of participants with the most efficient use of time.

Remember Why You're Doing What You're Doing

When you dramatically tell stories from the Scriptures, always strive to use your gifts and talents to the fullest. Worship and instruction in the faith deserve no less. Always keep in mind that when you perform a Gospeldrama you are not performing for the applause of the crowds; you perform to the glory of God as you try to help your listeners understand and remember the Gospel message.

I hope this chapter has given you enough ideas on the dramatic telling of a story to keep you going for at least a few weeks. By now you should be able to write simple echo pantomimes and Gospeldramas for almost any occasion. There is, however, another way of dramatically telling the story that we need to explore.

The next chapter will give you some ways to do ...

FIVE

Storytelling with Puppets

Use Puppets: They're Real

Each of us has had a favorite toy. When I was a little boy, I had a fuzzy, brown toy dog who was my constant companion. His name was Doggie. When I was four years old, I took him everywhere I went. I held him so much that he wore out in several places; so much so that my grandma had a full-time job just patching him up. One time she performed major surgery on Doggie. She used an old pair of socks to sew his head back onto his body. She told me that Doggie now wore a sweater to keep him warm. I accepted this without question. Doggie now had a nice blue sock, turtle neck sweater around the place where his neck used to be. Grandma had a great imagination. (It seems all grandparents do.)

Children cherish their toys. Sometimes they talk to them and tell them their deepest secrets. When we grow up, we no longer play with toy dogs or dolls. As we grow up, we sometimes let our imaginations hibernate. Children don't have that problem. Toys are real to them; they can hold a child's attention and captivate their imagination where we "real" people cannot.

When we use puppets to tell stories, we are meeting children where they live. We are reaching into their world of imagination. A puppet can often tell a story better than a real person because children relate to toys with ease. If you have ever talked to a toy yourself (now think back to when you were a child), you can qualify as a puppeteer. All you need is to get hold of a puppet and start talking through it. You don't have to be a ventriloquist. Your lips can move. All you have to do is hold up the puppet in front of the children and start to tell a story.

If you look at the puppet while you tell your story, a strange thing will happen. The puppet will develop a personality of its own. You will also be amazed that nobody will be looking at you. Everyone (children and adults) will be watching the puppet. They will be listening to it and not to you. You can be moving your lips like crazy and nobody will care. They will be too interested in listening to the story coming from the inanimate object you have mysteriously brought to life. But it's not magic; it takes work.

I have a favorite puppet. His name is The Bear, and he has delighted both me and my students for many years. He's pictured below in a number of classic poses for puppets. If you find a puppet that is a good fit, you will have no trouble imitating these poses. Practice the stock poses to add spice to your puppet acting. Some of the poses require some motion, but I think you will understand how they work as you try to imitate these pictures.

Stock Movements

The Bear

Prayer/Pleading
(*Hands/paws together*)

Anger
(*Shake with anger*)

Sadness/Sorrow
(*Hands/paws in front of eyes*)

Thinking
(*Scratch head with "paws"*)

Hello/Good-Bye
(*Wave hand*)

Calling/Whispering, or
Showing Surprise
(*Hands on sides of mouth*)

Take a Bow
(*Hand/paw to tummy, head
down to tummy*)

Joy
(*Quickly throw arms out*)

Other puppet actions for you to try:

Fear: Put puppet's hands on its head or in front of its mouth and shake puppet in short, jerky, nervous motion from front to back. Head of puppet should flop slightly forward and backward for best affect. Fear and anger actions are similar.

"Yes," or "I agree": Wiggle your index finger (in head of puppet) up and down.

"No," or "I disagree": Cross hands of puppet; keep puppet straight, and quickly twist your wrist right and left.

Yawn and Stretch: Arms go wide, while head tilts back as far as it can go.

Don't be fooled by the seemingly simplistic. Puppets are deceptively simple. Take time to practice these stock movements. As you learn to manipulate your puppets, you will be able to add a wide range of movements which will make the puppet live for your audience.

When you do movements with your puppet, remember it can move even if it's not "talking." When you direct a question to the puppet or if it is per-

forming with other puppets, it should react to what is said even if it isn't speaking. This is one of the hardest bits of business for puppeteers to perform, but with a little practice all these things will fall into place.

On the Making of Puppets and Puppet Theaters

In this chapter I will give you suggestions on how to make and use some selected types of puppets, show you a few simple types of puppet theaters that you can make, and suggest a simple set of box stages that you can use in conjunction with puppet theater and other dramatic presentations.

The types of puppets we'll look at are:

1. Hand Puppets (bought and homemade)
2. Spoon Puppets
3. Transparency Projected Puppets
4. Cut-out Puppets
5. Cardboard-Tube Puppets
6. Paper-Plate Puppets and Masks for Reader's Theater
7. Milk-Carton Puppets
8. Paper-Bag Puppets and Masks
9. Plastic Soft-Drink-Bottle Puppets
10. Sock Puppets
11. Finger Puppets
12. Potholder Puppets
13. Pop-Up Puppets

The types of stages we'll talk about are:
1. Bar and Curtain
2. Shadow Theater
3. Cardboard Refrigerator-Box Theater
4. Fancy, Wooden, Proscenium-Arch Theater with Curtains
5. Box Stages

But first, ask yourself the following

1. Am I good with a sewing machine?

If the answer is no, you may wish to enlist the help of a few sewing experts. If you have only modest skills with a sewing machine find someone who is a sewing wiz and ask them for help. Most simple puppets can be easily made with a sewing machine. Ask capable sewers to make a puppet far enough in advance, and they will be happy to come up with all sorts of wonderful puppets for you.

2. When was the last time I visited a fabric, craft, or hardware store, or a lumber yard, or a garage sale?

If you haven't been to a hardware, fabric, or craft store in the past six

months (or ever), you probably should take some time to do so.

Look for Popsicle sticks, glue, glitter, a hot glue gun (a most wonderful tool, especially for those of us who aren't too good with the sewing machine), paint stirring sticks (ask for a few from the paint store or hardware salesperson), dowels of various lengths and thicknesses, heavy duty stapler, assorted hinges, paint (tempera and others), paper bags (all sizes), yarn (assorted colors), crayons, cotton, buttons, nails/screws (assorted), 1/2″ or 3/4″ plywood, craft books on puppets.

You will probably have some things on the list at home. You will, however, probably need some help finding the more exotic things on the list.

Finally, don't forget that garage sales are ideal places to pick up both scrap materials, puppets, and other useful materials for teaching. Expensive puppets are often found for a quarter at a garage sale.

3. Is it what I know or who I know that's important?

Two important resources are 1) an expert crafter and 2) a Jack or Jill of all trades. Every church has at least one of each. Don't hesitate to ask them for their help. Knowing the human resources of your church and community is vital.

4. Do people I know have scrap materials lying around doing nothing?

A small ad placed in your church bulletin will probably bring more scrap cloth, yarn, socks, buttons, plywood, paint, hinges, and other assorted puppet making materials to you than you'll be able to use.

5. When is the last time I had a puppet-making party?

It's been about six years since I hosted a puppet-making party. From that one party I got enough puppets to last me for years. Invite some parents and teachers in your church to a puppet-making party. Invite some younger children and some teenagers; invite the crafters and the carpenters. Bring glue guns and sewing machines, scrap material and yarn, buttons and thread, paint and plywood. In one evening you will put together enough puppet resources to fill your puppet needs for years to come. Organize the party well. Specify the types of puppets you want to make and the kinds of puppet theaters you need to construct so your volunteers will know what needs to be done. When you have finished all the projects, have ice cream and cake.

6. What kinds of puppets should I make?

I usually suggest teachers have at least a dozen puppets at their disposal. A generic list of puppets might include:

A Mom

A Dad

An Older Son or Daughter

A Younger Son or Daughter

An Infant Son or Daughter

Several Children

Several Other Adults

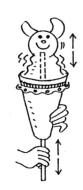

A Pet (dog and cat are favorites, but also consider a bird, goldfish, and turtle)

Some important Bible story characters such as: a Noah, who can also double as a Moses, Daniel, Wise Man, Joseph, or any prophet; and a Sarah, who can double as a Miriam, Ruth, Esther, Martha, Mary.

A Jesus puppet (should be distinct from other generic puppets)

Animal puppets such as lions, bears, wolves, pigs, donkeys, fish, and sheep.

Several imaginary puppets. Imaginary puppets are nondescript puppets that don't look like anything in particular. They are usually made up of leftover scraps. Imagine what they might be. If you're having trouble, think of Muppetlike characters for some ideas.

7. What about accessories?

One way to add interest to puppets is to add accessories such as hats, earrings, necklaces, ties, and other baubles to the costumes of your puppets. A few stops at a garage sale will provide you with all the accessories you need to dress up your characters. A little jewelry will go a long way in making your puppet characters come alive. Little hats for your puppets will accomplish the same thing. The personality of a puppet can be greatly changed with a little costuming.

8. Where should I keep my puppets after they're made?

Store puppets in a toy box, a sturdy cardboard box, plastic bins, and shoe boxes. (Be sure storage is accessible.) Shoe boxes provide inexpensive storage for puppets and other Sunday school materials. Shoe boxes are abundant, cheap, and easily labeled. More expensive storage cases (clear plastic boxes, for example) are wonderful if you have the money, but before you spend money on storage, think of using the money to buy the materials you need to make the stuff that you want to store. Shoe box storage is also good for rulers, scissors, glue sticks, tape, crayons, and all the other stuff that teachers need to do the job.

Puppets You Can Make

Actually, you can buy ready-made hand puppets in stores, but they are very expensive. Look for them instead at garage sales, and advertise in your church bulletin. Try to get hand-me-downs before buying them. Even so, there are times when puppets are on a to-good-to-miss sale. When that happens, get out your wallet and buy what you can afford.

When buying a ready-made puppet for your own use, look for one that seems to fit your hand the best. Sometimes puppets designed for children's hands don't work very well for adults.

I recommend, however, that you make your own puppets as a rule. For the same money, you'll have many more stock characters and you'll feel freer to modify them as the need arises.

Now—which will you make?

1. Hand Puppets (bought and homemade)

Hand puppet patterns can be purchased at most craft and fabric stores. Your craft store salesperson will help you select what you need to make all sorts of puppets and other homemade types of stuffed toys that can be used in a puppet theater. Here are some simple suggestions for puppets you and your children can make. Children should be engaged in designing and making puppets for use in class. When children have ownership of the puppets, they will want to use them more often and will be able to take them home and tell stories to their parents.

In order that all your children have ownership of the puppets, it is very important that you make puppets that are multicultural. Be sure that your puppets include Black, Hispanic, Asian, and Caucasian characters. Multi-cultural hand puppets can be purchased, but children will have more fun with their own homemade puppets. Crayola Corporation makes a set of eight washable, multicultural marking pens that are designed to help children more realistically color faces with true-to-life flesh tones. Make sure that you are multi-culturally inclusive as you design your puppets.

Here is a simple idea for felt/cloth hand puppets (plus one with a cheese box) you can make with your children:

2. Spoon Puppets

Spoon puppets are among the easiest to make. Purchase some wooden spoons from you local kitchen supply store or discount department store. Decorate the spoons with ribbon, yarn, construction paper, buttons, yarn, or magic markers.

3. Transparency-Projected Puppets

Transparency-projected puppets are easy to make, colorful, and can be easily seen by the audience. Here are the materials you will need to make and project them:

a. Clear write-on transparencies

b. A set of colored transparency marking pens (washable) or a set of colored laundry marking pens (permanent)

c. Some Popsicle sticks or other very thin sticks (dowels)

d. Cellophane tape

e. Scissors

f. An overhead projector

g. A projection screen; a white wall; or a king-size white sheet, stretched tightly over a square wooden frame.

Directions: Draw your characters on the clear transparencies. (Keep them small—2–3 inches wide and 3–5 inches high. Remember the overhead projection stage is only about a foot wide so you will not have lots of room for very large characters. Even though your characters are small, they will look large when you project them.) Color them as you like with either permanent or washable marking pens. Cut out your transparency drawings with a scissors. Tape a thin wooden stick (or a Popsicle stick that has been cut in half long ways) to the bottom of the cut out transparency figure. Hold puppets by the Popsicle stick or dowel and move them around as you project them.

For an interesting affect, try rear projection on a sheet. Rear projection is a way for you to show your transparency puppets (or any transparency for that matter) without being seen by the audience. If you put the projector behind a screen made from a king-size bed sheet, you can project your transparency puppets on the screen while you stay out of view of the audience. Remember if you project any words, you will have to flip the transparency so that the words will project correctly from the audience's point of view. You can do the same thing with slides, but remember: The slides will also have to be flipped in the projection tray so that they will read correctly to the audience. Don't flip them upside down—turn them around from right to left for proper projection. If all this seems confusing, don't worry. All you have to do is look at it from the audience's point of view and everything will become clear. Check the diagrams below for examples of how to do it.

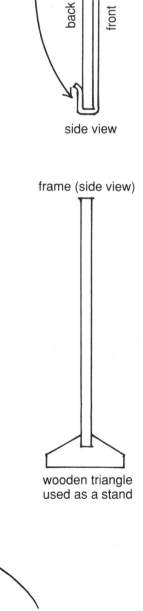

sheet stretched around frame

staple here

back

front

side view

frame (side view)

wooden triangle used as a stand

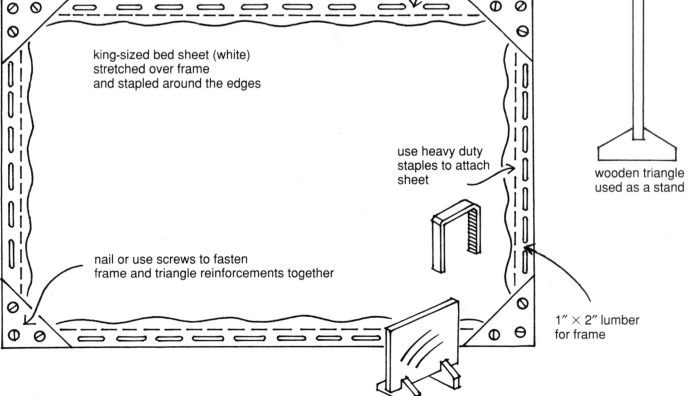

king-sized bed sheet (white) stretched over frame and stapled around the edges

use heavy duty staples to attach sheet

nail or use screws to fasten frame and triangle reinforcements together

1" × 2" lumber for frame

You can also use silhouette images for projection on a screen with an overhead projector. All you need is cut-out shapes that, when projected, will form a black silhouette image on the screen. You can front or rear project these images as you wish. See examples:

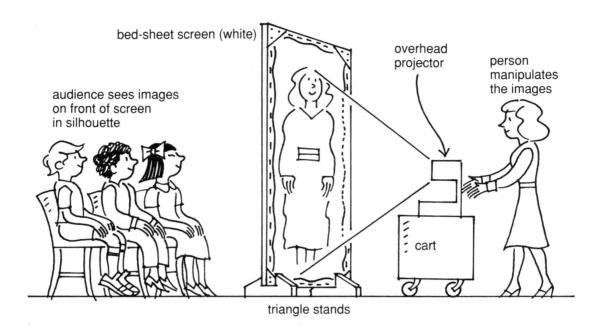

Note: For more information, see Chapter 9, "The Overhead Projector and Transparencies," page 113.

Another tip about using overhead projections:

Sometimes it is a good practice to set up your silhouette images on the "stage" of the overhead projector with the lamp off. Then turn on the overhead as you start to tell the story. When the next scene is ready to be projected, turn the overhead lamp off and set up the next scene before you turn the lamp on again. This revealing technique gives the audience a surprise as they watch the silhouette-puppets cut-outs perform their shadow play.

Sometimes an assistant can do the set-ups and projection for you while you tell the story. If you can rehearse this with someone a bit before the performance, you will find that the audience will be highly engaged in the story. If you are able to rear project the silhouettes with an assistant who is behind the screen, the story will be even more exciting.

Yet another tip about using overhead rear projection:

This is not a puppet technique, but as long as we're talking about rear projection and silhouettes I want to mention that actors can also be projected using a similar rear projection technique.

Directions: Place an overhead projector between the actors and screen. Turn the overhead projector lamp on and have the actors pose behind the screen so that their shadows fall on the screen. Actors should stand fairly close to screen so the shadows are crisp. Actors may also perform movements but must be careful not to upstage each other's shadows.

This type of shadow play is a good way to get children involved in the dramatic telling of the story because they will not be overcome with stage fright. In fact, they will never have to see the audience face to face when they perform a shadow play. They will, however, be able to see exactly what their shadow looks like on their side of the screen so that they can adjust their movements to get just the right shadow effects. I highly recommend the shadow play to you as a way of involving students of all ages and all ranges of talent in the dramatic telling of the story.

4. Cut-Out Puppets

Cut-out puppets are simply people, animals, and objects that are cut out of cardboard and decorated with paint, construction paper, crayons, etc. These puppets are then mounted on a stick. Use some thin wooden strips or paint-stirring sticks. (Paint-stirring sticks can be decorated to make puppets too.) Once mounted on the sticks, puppets can be held above the stage with ease. It is important to use cardboard for the characters so they don't flop around or easily rip when you are acting with them. Draw the face on both sides of the cut out puppet so that they can face in different directions.

5. Cardboard-Tube Puppets

Cardboard-tube puppets are fun and easy to make. They are also very inexpensive and can be made with cardboard toilet paper and paper towel tubes. Here's what you need to make them:

1. Cardboard toilet paper, paper towel, Christmas wrapping and/or other kinds of cardboard tubes. (I like cardboard-tube puppets because they let you recycle something that you normally throw away and use lots of scraps that otherwise would go into the garbage. By the way, I have kept some of my cardboard-tube puppets in shoe boxes and reused them for years.)

2. Construction paper in assorted colors (to wrap around the tubes to add color, clothing, etc.). Construction paper can also be used to make arms and hands that can be glued to the puppet.

3. Glue stick, tape, and/or staples. Staples can be used to affix construction paper because the stapler can be easily inserted into the tubes up to about four inches.

4. Yarn for hair and for tying on headgear.

5. Scrap flannel or any other fabric for making clothes, hats, etc.

6. Colored pens, pencils, glitter, multicultural Crayola marking pens, crayons, glitter, aluminum foil (great for simulating armor), and other decorations.

7. Stiff cardboard strips for making stronger arms.

8. Scissors or single-edge razor blade for cutting slits into cardboard tubes (insert stiff cardboard strips through the tube for stronger arms when necessary). Watch out with the razor blades with children, of course!

Here are some examples:

The birth of Jesus: Characters include baby Jesus, Mary, Joseph, Wise Men, angel(s), and shepherds (sheep optional).

Note: Fasten two long paper towel tubes together with masking tape and put a character at each end. By using a longer tube you won't have to stretch so much to get the puppet over the edge of the puppet stage.

Easter morning at the empty tomb: Characters include Mary Magdalene, Mary the mother of James, some other women, angel, Roman guards, Peter, John, Jesus.

Daniel in the lion's den: Characters include Daniel, King Darius, assorted administrators and satraps (i.e., the bad guys), several lions, and an angel.

6. Paper-Plate Puppets and Masks for Reader's Theater

Paper-plate puppets are made with paper plates and sticks. Put your creativity to use and decorate them as you wish. See examples below:

back view

Another tip for using paper-plate puppets: Paper-plate puppets can easily be turned into masks and used in a Reader's Theater setting. The paper plate (now a mask) can be held in front of actors' faces while they read their parts. Usually the mask is raised when the characters are speaking and lowered when they are not. Actors can be seated on stools or can stand as they read their parts.

Actors may be elevated on stools so they will be more easily seen by the audience. Scripts can be placed on music stands that can be adjusted for both height and tilt. When scripts are on music stands, the actors have one hand free to turn pages or gesture while holding their mask with the other. Cut a small mouth opening in the paper-plate mask (or any mask) so the actors' voices won't be muffled as they speak.

7. Milk-Carton Puppets

Milk cartons (orange-juice cartons, etc.) come in several sizes, making them usable with every size hand; pint size for little children, quart size for middle-size children, and half-gallon size for older children and adults. Here's an example of how to make one. Don't forget to thoroughly rinse milk cartons.

Suggested materials: milk cartons (any size), stapler, glue, construction paper, colored marking pens, crayons, buttons (for eyes), yarn (for hair), felt or other cloth material (for clothes), discarded ties, hats, earrings, masking or cellophane tape, scissors or utility knife (not for little children), old socks (to hide your bare arm and act as clothing for the puppet).

8. Paper-Bag Puppets and Masks

Paper bags also come in small, medium, and large sizes and can be used as puppets or masks.

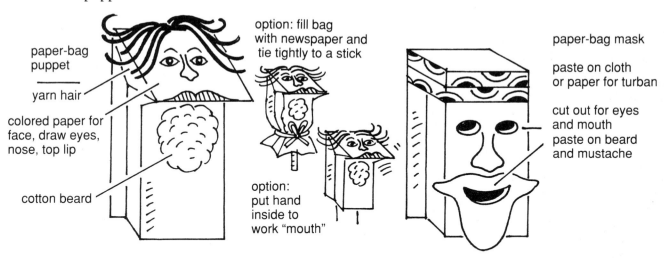

paper-bag puppet

yarn hair

colored paper for face, draw eyes, nose, top lip

cotton beard

option: fill bag with newspaper and tie tightly to a stick

option: put hand inside to work "mouth"

paper-bag mask

paste on cloth or paper for turban

cut out for eyes and mouth
paste on beard and mustache

9. Plastic Soft-Drink-Bottle Puppets

Materials: Two liter, plastic, soft-drink bottles, cardboard toilet-paper tubes, paper bags (sandwich size), scrap cloth material, stapler, yarn (for hair as always), cotton for beards, construction paper (for use anywhere you like), cardboard (for making shoes), filament tape (the kind with plastic coating that's used for taping boxes for shipment—really sturdy and will not rip like masking tape), masking or cellophane tape (for use in places where ripping is not a problem), colored marking pens or crayons, Styrofoam ball or other roundish material for a head, paint-stirring stick or wooden dowel.

Directions: Take a plastic, soft-drink bottle and rinse it thoroughly. Use cardboard toilet-paper tubes for arms and legs. Attach arms and legs with filament tape to plastic body. Attach a paint stick or wooden dowel to the body, or use two strings to turn the puppet into a marionettelike figure. Wrap cardboard tubes with cloth or construction paper for pants and shirt sleeves. Use paper bag as suit or dress (color as desired). Attach cardboard feet or shoes to legs with tape or staples. Make a head from a Styrofoam ball or stuff cloth or old pantyhose with newspaper to make a roundish head. Paint or color face on head with marking pens, or crayons. Here's an example:

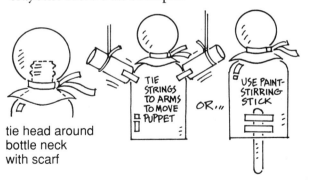

tie head around bottle neck with scarf

TIE STRINGS TO ARMS TO MOVE PUPPET

OR

USE PAINT-STIRRING STICK

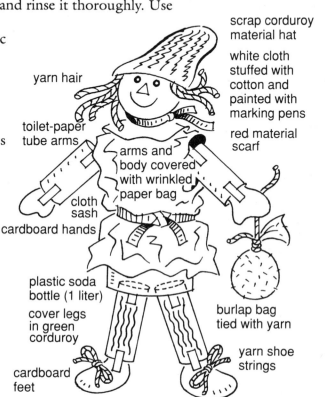

scrap corduroy material hat

white cloth stuffed with cotton and painted with marking pens

red material scarf

yarn hair

toilet-paper tube arms

arms and body covered with wrinkled paper bag

cloth sash

cardboard hands

plastic soda bottle (1 liter)

cover legs in green corduroy

cardboard feet

burlap bag tied with yarn

yarn shoe strings

10. Sock Puppets

Sock puppets are some of the most popular puppets that children can make. They are simple, easy to use, and can be made from something that everyone has—a sock without a mate!

Materials: Socks (any color, any kind), buttons (for eyes) or plastic eyes that you can buy from the craft store (these are neat because the pupils of the eyes can roll around as you move the puppet's head).

11. Finger Puppets

Finger puppets are especially useful with small children. Finger puppets can be made in several ways. They can be crocheted and placed over the fingers.

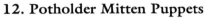

They can be made by attaching small faces to fingers with tape.

They can be made by attaching small faces to glove fingers.

See the Resource List on page 00 for more ideas on finger puppets.

12. Potholder Mitten Puppets

Potholder mittens (made in the likeness of cows, pigs, and other animals) can be purchased in stores or can be made by using ordinary potholder mittens. Simply take the potholder glove and dress it in some fabric. Add button eyes, and a few strokes of colored marking pens, some accessories, and you have a great puppet. The thumb of the mitten becomes the lower jaw of the puppet.

13. Pop-Up Puppets

Pop-up puppets are made with a dowel, a piece of fabric, a cone-shaped piece of cardboard or cup, and a small ball made of wood, Styrofoam, or rubber. They are fun to make and to use because they provide a surprise when they pop up out of their hiding place (the cone or cup). Here is an example of how you can make one. One performance tip: Pop-up and twist to look from side to side to look around.

Puppet Stages You Can Make

Puppet stages are important because they allow the audience to focus more of their attention on the puppets. When the puppeteers are hidden behind a curtain or wall, more complex action can take place. Actors can easily read their scripts and communicate with each other more efficiently behind the puppet curtain. Stages also make a performance something special. The stage itself (even a simple one) signals to the audience that they should pay special attention to what is happening next. When we set the stage, we are helping our listeners to be attentive and to listen with care as the drama unfolds.

Bar and Curtain

The simplest type of stage you can make is the "bar and curtain." All you need is a large piece of fabric, a clothing bar or long piece of 1″ × 2″ lumber (between 5–10 feet long), and two people to hold the bar and curtain. Here is an example:

The fabric should not have a busy pattern. A solid color such as blue, gray, or purple will be much better than a bright red or striped pattern. Wild patterns and striking colors may distract your viewers. The fabric should be lightweight, but opaque enough to hide the actors. Sound will penetrate thinner material better than thick, plush fabrics. Using lightweight materials will also help your curtain-holding stage crew to keep from getting cramps in their arms (especially important for younger children).

Another tip: Pin or tape your script to the back of the curtain so that your puppeteers can have their hands free to manipulate the puppets. This also saves them the trouble of turning the pages of the script while their hands are full.

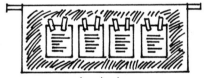

Cardboard Refrigerator-Box Theater

Go to your local appliance store and ask for a washing machine box or, better yet, a refrigerator box. A refrigerator box makes a great puppet theater. See directions below.

A few tips:

1. Because a refrigerator box can only hold one or two people, you must be careful to choose or write puppet plays that can be done with a minimum number of puppets.

2. Drape a piece of cloth over the back of the box as a backdrop. Scenery can also be taped or pinned to the backdrop.

3. If you use a white sheet for a backdrop, you can rear project a 35mm color slide on the sheet as scenery. For example, take some pictures

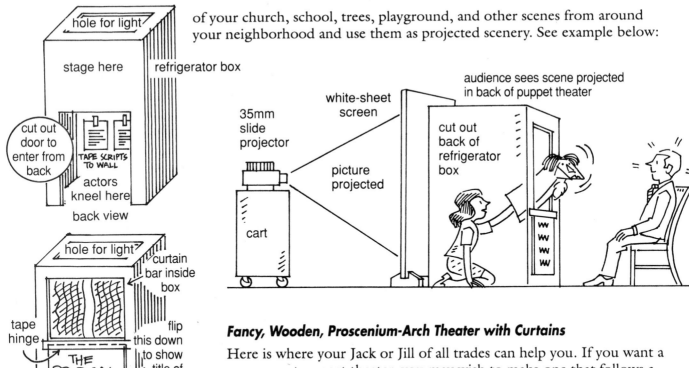

of your church, school, trees, playground, and other scenes from around your neighborhood and use them as projected scenery. See example below:

Fancy, Wooden, Proscenium-Arch Theater with Curtains

Here is where your Jack or Jill of all trades can help you. If you want a more permanent puppet theater, you may wish to make one that follows a design like the one below. This kind of theater is semiportable and can be stored flat against the wall when folded. A curtain can be hung across the front of the stage and you can do the same type of rear projection on a backdrop as you did in the refrigerator-box style theater. The advantage of a wooden or masonite theater is that you can house more than one or two puppeteers at a time. Here is a diagram of a semiportable theater:

Box Stages

Every church should have a set of at least three stage boxes. Stage boxes are versatile platforms arranged in a number of ways to help actors see the audience and vice versa. They can be used behind puppet theaters to help elevate shorter children and are useful in almost any performance situation. They can double as the choir director's podium or as risers for a choir. They are made from ¾″ plywood in square, rectangular, or triangular shapes. Here are some basic designs and stage layouts that you can use as you tell stories.

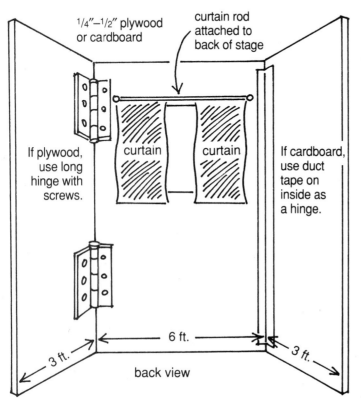

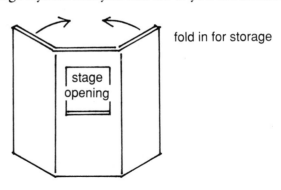

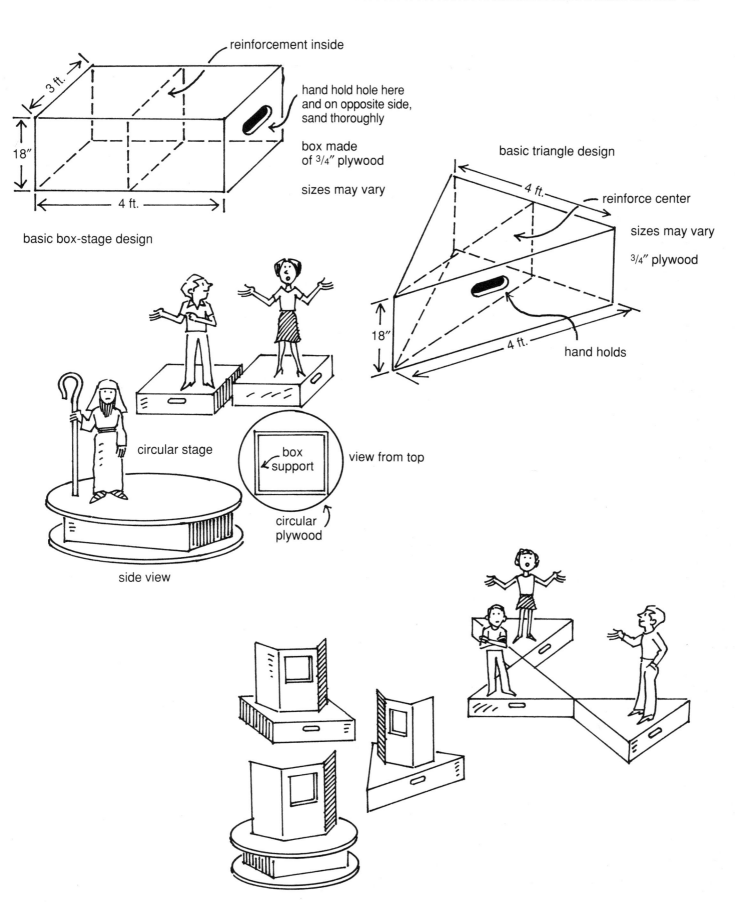

reinforcement inside

3 ft.

18"

4 ft.

basic box-stage design

hand hold hole here
and on opposite side,
sand thoroughly

box made
of 3/4" plywood

sizes may vary

basic triangle design

4 ft.

reinforce center

sizes may vary

3/4" plywood

18"

4 ft.

hand holds

circular stage

box
support

view from top

circular
plywood

side view

You're Ready to Move On

God's blessings as you dramatically tell the stories to children through puppeteering! Remember that puppets are living things to children—and you are the one who will make them live.

Now, on to the next chapter, which not only has many applications for telling the story dramatically but other uses as well. It's something that is becoming less and less common today. It's something that was once held in high esteem and greatly valued. It's something that most people don't like to do, but need to be able to do at one time or another. It's called ...

Memorization

Nothing strikes terror in the hearts of students more than the word *memorization*. I remember when I was assigned a poem, Bible passage, hymn stanza, or a catechism explanation to memorize. There were always some kids in my class who seemed to be able to memorize without any effort. They were always at the front of the line to do their recitation and had their hand up first when the teacher asked, "Who remembers the Bible passage for today." I always tried to hide behind the kid who had her hand up. When my hiding strategy didn't work, I quickly started raising my hand in the hope that I would not be noticed amid all the other waving hands. My teacher immediately called upon me. I just couldn't win.

To my embarrassment I was often found wanting when it came time for me to recite my memory work. I began to hate it. (If I would have spent as much time memorizing as I did thinking about how much I hated memorizing, I would have had the whole Bible down by heart.)

I developed other strategies to get me through the memory assignment. I remember how I would cram right before I went to take my turn in the memory line at the teacher's desk. I got the words out (good short term memory), but they were gone from my mind by the time I got back to my desk. Cramming was a short-term solution that only led to long-term frustration.

Something happened to me, however, by the time I got to seventh or eighth grade; I began to memorize things with greater ease. By the time I was in high school, memorization, while still a chore, was not as difficult as it had been. I no longer hated it. I even tried out for plays (you've got to memorize there) and seemed to have less and less difficulty with the larger portions of memorization that I had to do. Part of this, I'm sure, was due to maturity, but I believe that something else also happened. The big difference came when memory was *taught* and not merely assigned. In this chapter you will find ideas, strategies, and games that I have found useful in teaching memory work.

Before You Assign Memory Work

My first teaching experience was with third and fourth graders. I resolved that I would *teach* them memory work and not merely assign it to them. I didn't want my students to have the same bad memories that I had. In essence, I used the same strategy for memory that I have outlined regarding pre-preparation or writing echo pantomime: break things down into smaller parts, analyze them, and then put them back together in a new way.

But before I started *teaching* memory work, I asked myself a number of questions.

1. Why should the children memorize this passage?

Why is this particular passage important to commit to memory? What truth does it teach? How does it proclaim the Gospel? Why have other people memorized this passage? Do you believe the passage is worthy of memorization, or are you just assigning it to the children because the book tells you to? Questions such as these help you to focus on why the passage is important and how you will go about teaching its significance to your students.

2. Am *I* willing to commit this passage to memory?

Few teaching strategies or methods are as powerful as modeling. If you assign something to be memorized you should memorize the passage yourself. Why should children believe that a passage is important if you haven't committed it to memory? If you assign it, you memorize it. (I hope that this doesn't kill off all memory work now, but I really believe that it is essential for you to model this behavior for your children. Besides, you will have a little more empathy for them and gain a better understanding of the passage as you teach for memory.)

3. Do I quote passages from memory that relate to my life *now*?

When you quote passages that you have memorized and talk about why they are important to you, you will show children the importance of the Bible passage. I remember one person saying to me, "You'll be glad to know this passage when you're on your deathbed. It will be of great comfort to you then."

Children don't usually think about memorizing passages for use that far down the road. If passages only promise comfort far in the distant future, it is unlikely they will be given much serious thought in the present. As you quote passages that are important to you now, you will be teaching children that Scripture is alive and meaningful in the present.

4. Have I taught the memory work thoroughly *before* making the assignment?

I try never to let my students know what they're doing until they've done it—then they can't say they can't do it or don't understand it. When I teach memory work, I don't always tell the children that the passage they're working with will be assigned as memory. First I teach—then I assign. Most students catch on to my strategy pretty fast, but they play the game because they know that they will be more successful at remembering the assignment that is bound to come.

5. Is repetition the same as teaching?

An old Latin saying goes like this: *Repetitio est mater studiorum* ("Repetition is the mother of learning"). Most of us have to repeat something several times if we want to memorize it. But mere repetition is no insurance we will memorize anything. A passage quoted perfectly, but not understood or internalized, is only a "vain repetition" (as in "But when you pray, use not vain repetitions, as the heathen do: for they think that they shall be heard for their much speaking" (Matthew 6:7, KJV).

Most memory work will need to be repeated a number of times, but it is more important that we teach the meaning of passages, hymn stanzas, catechism explanations, and other memory work that we assign. A Bible passage or hymn stanza will have a better chance of being memorized if it is meaningful. Teaching the meaning of a passage *precedes* memory. When passages have significant personal meaning to children, they will be remembered with much less effort.

6. Have I given the children the opportunity to choose their own passages for recitation?

At the start of your class, take a few moments to ask children to share one of their favorite Bible passages or hymn stanzas with the rest of the class. When children are allowed to choose their own passages, they will be more successful in remembering them. They also will be more willing to share the reasons why these passages are significant to them. This kind of activity is especially useful with older children. Try to find time in your lesson to have children express their own feelings about passages that are significant to them.

Some Techniques for Teaching Memory Work

These techniques for teaching memory work can be used with children from grade 3 and up. Modify some for younger children.

1. Look at every word of the passage to make sure that children understand the basic vocabulary.

In this passage the words in **bold type** might need explanation or definition.

> Be **sober**, be **vigilant**, because your **adversary** the devil, as a roaring lion, walketh about, seeking whom he may **devour** (1 Peter 5:8, KJV).

I like this version of the passage because it is familiar to me and I like the Shakespearean walketh and talketh style of writing. Unfortunately, most people don't talketh like that any more. What is clear, familiar, and understandable to you may be very confusing to others—especially children. Define unfamiliar vocabulary no matter which translation of the Bible you use. Don't assume that a translation will be understood just because it's "modern." Here's the same passage in the NIV.

> Be **self-controlled** and **alert**. Your enemy the devil **prowls** around like a roaring lion looking for someone to **devour**" (1 Peter 5:8).

As you can see, you may need to define words no matter what the translation. The words *self-controlled* or *alert* may not be understood by every child. What does "prowls" mean? Would all students know? Could they all figure out what words mean within the context they are written? Spend at least of few minutes reviewing words you think might present problems. A dictionary of the English language and a Bible dictionary will help you to thoroughly define and describe words, interpret customs, and explain other parts of the passage that may be problematic.

2. Use different translations to help you understand the vocabulary before assigning memory work.

By comparing several versions of the same passage, you will help students (and yourself) to define and comprehend the meaning of the passage. The more the meaning is understood, the easier it will be to memorize.

3. Keep the passage in front of their eyes as much as you can.

Write the passage on the chalkboard before class so that everyone can see it throughout the period. Children will start to memorize the passage without even knowing that they are doing it if they see it before their eyes.

4. Read the passage aloud several times during the course of the class period.

You can read it and they can read it as well. You don't have to read it a dozen times, but you should feel free to refer to the passage whenever necessary. Depending on its length, you will probably repeat the entire passage or phrases of the passage several times during the course of the lesson. Hearing the spoken word is another way to reinforce memory.

Use these first four suggestions during *every* memory teaching session. They are essential for teaching the memory assignment. To summarize: Define the vocabulary, compare translations, see the passage, hear the passage spoken aloud.

More Memory Strategies

1. Bible passage jigsaw puzzle.

Write the passage on a piece of thin cardboard. Cut the words into a jigsaw puzzle. Individual students or groups of students can put them together. The jigsaw pieces can be simple or complex, depending on the length of the passage and the age level of the students. Try having your students write out the passage and cut it into a puzzle. Students can then trade their puzzles with each other. Put each puzzle in an envelope and keep them for future use. Use to review the memory work or as a pre-class activity for future classes. Send the puzzles home to be worked on with parents.

2. Put the words of the passage on 3″ × 5″ cards.

This is a modification of the jigsaw idea. Write words on individual cards. Mix them. Give each child a card. Ask children to stand in a line in the correct order to construct the passage. Have the children tack the passage on the bulletin board—then scramble and unscramble the words. Leave the correct version on the board through the period. Play a concentration game with the cards by turning them over and guessing which card comes first, second, third, etc. until you have the passage complete. Use any kind of cards you want (old business cards or throw-away paper). Put the cards in an envelope for future use. Write the Bible passage (book, chapter, and verse) on the outside of the envelope for reference. Store your Bible-passage cards in a shoe box for future use.

3. Use individual chalkboards to write and say passages.

One of the easiest ways to display the Bible passage is to use individual chalkboards. Make individual chalkboards out of one-foot-square pieces of

Masonite painted with chalkboard paint (see Chapter 7, page 105, for details). Have children write each word of the passage on the chalkboards and then put them in order in a similar way as you did with the 3″ × 5″ cards. The advantage to using a chalkboard is that the words can be made larger and you can erase and use the boards again and again. Scrap or recycled paper can also be used for the same purpose.

4. Fill in the blanks.

Put the passage on an overhead projection transparency, but leave out selected words. Project the transparency and have students try to fill in the blanks as you teach the passage. Here's an example:

> For God _____ loved the _____, that he gave his _____ begotten Son, that whosoever believeth in him should not _____, but have _____ life. (John 3:16, KJV)

This could also be done on the chalkboard or on individual chalkboards. The variations are many, but the idea is the same.

5. Cooperative exercises

As students learn to read and understand passages on their own, give them the opportunity to interpret and explain the passage to each other. Break your class into groups of three or four students (groups of more than four are probably too large for most cooperative exercises) and try a cooperative exercise such as this:

1. Break into random groups by counting off or by picking numbers from a hat.

2. Each member of the group should have a copy of the passage.

3. Assign a role to each of the students in the group as follows:

    a. The Reader: Reads the passage aloud to rest of group as they listen. The Reader tries to read the passage carefully so that the listeners really pay attention to what's being read.

    b. Recorder: Writes down a few words that each member of the group will supply.

    c. A Questioner: Asks other members for clarification of their statements. The Questioner figures out when the group is going off task and tries to bring them back on target. The Questioner says things such as, "I don't think everyone understands what you mean, could you repeat that?"

    d. The Encourager: Listens carefully as people speak and tries to point out good. The Encourager says things such as, "That's a good idea," or "I appreciate what you just said." All people can encourage and question at any time, the assignment of different roles is an attempt to make sure that someone covers the bases. Having everyone take a role also helps to maximize participation. If you have a group of three, you can double up on role assignments.

4. Have the groups follow these instructions:

    a. Have the Readers read the passage quietly to their group. (This will

sound a little funny, because they will all start reading about the same time. Don't let that stop the activity—just recognize that it will happen and go on.)

b. Each member of the group will take a little silent time to read the passage to themselves after the Reader has read it. Each group member will select three or four words from the passage that they think are the most important words for understanding the passage. No comments will be made by anyone regarding the words.

c. The Recorder will record each of the words on a piece of paper. Some words may be the same—that's okay.

d. Once the words are recorded, each member will take a turn explaining why they chose the words they chose and why they think they are significant to the meaning of the passage. The emphasis here is on sharing and explaining, not on correct or incorrect answers.

e. When everyone has had a turn explaining why they feel their words are important, the group will decide on which three words are most important to an understanding of the passage and come to some agreement as to why they are most important. This is not a competition to see whose words are better than others but a meeting of minds regarding which words are most important. (Again, don't dwell on right and wrong answers.)

f. Once the group has agreed on their three words, they should elect someone to report back to the rest of the groups. The Reporter should be ready to tell what the words are and why they are important to understanding the passage.

5. As each group reports, you can make a master list of important words on the chalkboard. As you discuss the meaning of the words, try to involve as many students as possible. Often independent groups will come up with the same most important words. When this happens, you have a neat opportunity for discussion.

When you are finished with the exercise, you (and the students) will be surprised at how well they know the passage. The children will have read the passage many times during their discussion and will have concentrated on it in depth. Once they have done that, they will be well on their way to memorizing it. (Incidentally, this is also a good way for adults to study Bible passages and stories.)

6. Tape record Bible passages.

Children love to hear each other on tape. They enjoy putting their voice on tape and listening to it. When children listen to passages they have recorded, it reinforces their learning and helps them memorize. They will be able to anticipate the words, follow them on the printed page, and repeat them correctly. Since many children have access to audiocassette tape recorders at home, this activity is easy to do. Children can also keep a running account of their memory work.

Suggest children make an audiocassette tape "journal" of each passage. After reciting a passage, the children and their parents can comment on

what the passage means to them. Children and parents (grandparents will love this as well) can listen in years to come. A video tape recording can also serve the same purpose.

Make memory tapes for your students. This is an excellent opportunity for teachers to communicate the meaning of passages to both students and their parents. It is also another opportunity for teachers to communicate with students *and* parents through another medium.

A brief tape-recorded message and Bible passage is another way to inform parents about what is happening in the class.

Remember that Each Child Is Different

Every student in your class is different. Some of them will find memorization a breeze and others will literally be horrified by it. Some children love to recite in front of their peers and others will be petrified at the mere thought of speaking publicly. (A recent poll showed that many people are more afraid of speaking in public than they are of death.)

Always take individual differences into account when working with children. Some children will need more time to memorize a passage than others. That doesn't mean they are lazy or uninterested, it means that they are different. Give children every opportunity to memorize at their own speed. It is better to internalize, understand, and remember 10 passages than to recite 50 without understanding.

Memorization takes patience on the part of the learner and the teacher. Given time, most students will be successful memorizers. By devoting sufficient time to teaching memory work, you will help all students remember not only the words, but the meaning behind the words as well. In this way you will be teaching more than memory work, you will be teaching the faith.

The following chapters are designed to give you some helpful multimedia instructional tools and techniques. The next chapter deals with …

SEVEN

Individual Chalkboards

One of the easiest and most practical low-tech instructional tools you can make or purchase is an individual chalkboard. Chalkboards (or slates, as they used to be called) were commonplace in classrooms of the past. They are enjoyable to use and are a good alternative to paper.

You can purchase small individual chalkboards at your local school supply store. If they don't have them in stock, they will be able to order them for you. However, most store-bought chalkboards are small and flimsy. They are easily broken and often a little too small.

Make Your Own Chalkboards

1. Purchase a 4′ × 8′ sheet of ¼″ masonite at your local building supply store.

2. Cut the masonite sheet into as many as 32 one-foot squares. Find someone in your congregation who has a table saw. They will be happy to help you out if I know carpenter-type people. Save what you don't need for another project.

3. Ask your local paint dealer for some chalkboard paint (black or green). This paint usually comes in pint and quart sizes.

4. Paint the *smooth* side of your foot-square masonite boards as follows: Apply one coat of paint with an up-and-down stroke of your brush. Allow it to dry thoroughly. Apply a second coat with a side-to-side stroke of your brush. Allow to dry thoroughly. You don't want to write on it until the surface has dried hard! Don't try to rush the drying process.

   Avoid streaks by an even application of the paint. Because chalkboard paint is a little expensive, paint only one side of your chalkboards to stretch your dollar.

5. Purchase a plastic milk carton box at your local discount store and store your chalkboards in it. They should fit perfectly (you might want to measure the inside dimension of the carton just to be on the safe side.

6. Purchase a couple of boxes of hypo-allergenic, dustless chalk.

7. Ask your congregation members (through your church bulletin) or your students to bring an old sock to class. The socks make perfect erasers. Put a piece of chalk in each sock, and you have a combination chalk holder/eraser.

Using Individual Chalkboards

1. Distribute the chalkboards as efficiently as possible.

Lots of class time is wasted through inefficient distribution of materials. If you are going to use chalkboards during your lesson, it is probably a good idea to have them distributed to the children before class starts. The chalkboard, socks, and chalk should be ready to go when you get to the part of your lesson that calls for their use.

Note: The more you prepare these nuts-and-bolts management items (material distribution, attendance, offering collection, devotion schedule, clean-up helpers, and routines, etc.), the more smoothly your lesson will go. Thinking about how you perform your classroom management routines should be a part of your lesson pre-preparation (see Chapter 3, Step 9, "Finalize the Lesson," p. 33.

2. Use them as memory cards.

Use chalkboards as "memory game" cards. Have students write each word of the memory verse on a separate chalkboard. You can mix and match them, hold each word up as the verse is spoken, use them in a concentration game, and display them in correct order in the chalk rack of your blackboard. Almost any memory card game can be played using individual chalkboards.

3. Use them to draw pictures.

Many activities in religious curricula call for children to draw pictures. Often these pictures are done with crayon on paper that later ends up in the waste can. Use chalkboards on occasion as a substitute for crayon and paper drawings.

4. Use them as name cards for introductions.

Have children print their names on the chalkboards as they introduce themselves to the class. They might draw a picture of something that is meaningful to them as an ice breaker for their introduction. The chalkboard name cards can help you to get to know them better.

5. Use chalkboards during free time.

When children are filtering into class, give each a chalkboard on which to draw. They may wish to just draw, or you might give them something specific to do with their drawings that will relate to some part of your lesson.

6. Have students write memory verses on the chalkboard.

A chalkboard can be substituted for almost any activity that uses paper and pencil. Rather than have children write their memory verse on paper, consider the chalkboard as an alternative.

7. Make a chalkboard mural.

If you have ever worked through a crossword puzzle book, you probably have done a Skill-O-Gram. A Skill-O-Gram presents you with a number of squares that contain parts of a larger picture. When you copy them and put the smaller pieces together in the right order, you get to see a complete picture. You can use chalkboards to do this kind of puzzle picture. When you put all the pieces of the puzzle (chalkboards) together, the whole picture will emerge. Here's an example of how you might do it:

a. Take a simple picture from your student workbook and cut it into as many squares as you have children in your class.

b. Give each of your students one of the cut-out picture squares and have them copy the lines of the miniature picture on their chalkboard so as to make an enlargement of their picture.

c. Put the chalkboard pieces into the correct order, and you will create an enlarged mural of the original picture.

Note: I have done this activity with older children who have used colored chalk to do their drawings. When the puzzle is put together, the results can be striking and worthy of display.

8. Maintenance hint.

When your chalkboards get dirty, wash them with a damp cloth. Do not get them too wet, especially the unpainted back. Avoid over-washing your chalkboards; they only need it once in a while.

Some More Low-Tech Teaching Tools

Other low-tech teaching tools which both you and the children will enjoy using to tell the story are ...

EIGHT

Flannelboards, Display Boards, and Other Flannel Materials

Flannelboards are easy to make and use. The basic technique for their use is no different from that used in telling stories with puppets or pictures. The principles are the same, but the medium is different. The most important thing to remember when working with flannelboards is to put the pieces in sequence so that you don't have to hunt for them as you tell the story.

A Simple Flannel Display Board

Here are several simple designs for flannelboards you can make. You can make a flannelboard any size you want. However, keep them small for ease in storing and carrying.

Make sure the flannelboard is angled to keep pieces from falling off.

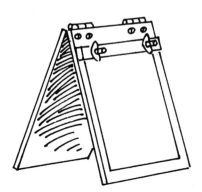
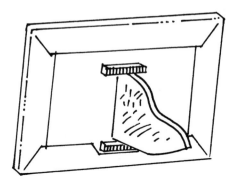

Keep pieces as flat as possible. Wrinkles and deep creases in flannel/felt pieces make them less sticky. Avoid using felt pieces too small to pick up. If the pieces are too small to pick up, they will probably be too small to be easily seen by the children. If the flannel character will not stay on the board, try rolling up a small piece of masking tape and apply it to the back of the character. In most cases the masking tape will be sticky enough to hold the flannel piece to the board.

Standard Characters, Props, and Scenery

Flannel cut-outs are easy to make. You can trace picture patterns from your student workbooks, coloring books, picture books, Arch Books® (see resource section), or create patterns freehand. Avoid using bright colors for flannelboard backgrounds. Save the bright colors for your characters, props, and scenery. A neutral color such as gray or light blue usually works well for

flannelboard backgrounds.

Here are some standard flannel/felt cut-outs that every teacher's resource room should have:

Set One: Adam, Eve, tree of good and evil, serpent, angel with sword.

Set Two: Noah and his relatives, the ark, water with waves, a variety of animals, Mt. Ararat, an altar, clouds with rain, rainbow.

Set Three: Abraham, Isaac, Sarah, ram, bushes, altar, rope, knife.

Set Four: David, Goliath, assorted Philistines and Israelites, sling, stones, King Saul, armor, long spear, extras (tents, sheep).

Set Five: Daniel, lions and lion's den, king, three men in furnace, angel, assorted evil characters.

Set Six: Jesus and disciples, fishing boat, loaves and fishes, water and waves, temple, Wise Men, manger, shepherds, angels, empty tomb with stone, three crosses, Jesus on cross with thieves, Pilate, Herod, assorted Pharisees, teachers of the law, lame man, ten lepers.

Here are a few patterns for you to use:

As you can see, many of the characters will be interchangeable. Once you have made a few generic characters, you can use them in a variety of different stories. Feel free to add facial features and other coloring to your flannel characters with permanent fine-tipped marking pens.

Try to keep your flannel board stories in separate plastic Zip-Lock bags. Plastic bags are good to use because you can easily see what's inside.

Once you have your flannel/felt characters and props, you can display them on the flannel board, bulletin board, or flannel apron.

Other Approaches to Consider

Flannel Aprons and Shirts

If you are handy with a sewing machine, (or if you can work a glue gun), you might try making a flannel apron. Buy an inexpensive apron at your discount store and cover it with flannel or felt material. When you put on the apron, you can attach the characters to the apron as you speak. You may be a bit limited in your movements, but you will be able to face your class as you tell the story. I have also used a black sweat shirt turned inside out as a flannelgraph shirt.

When I tell stories with such an apron or shirt, I try to keep the story as simple as I can. I try not to have more than two or three flannel pieces on the apron or shirt at a time. Remember to use dark materials in your flannel shirts and aprons.

Velcro Dots and Snaps

Velcro dots and strips are also very good to use in making flannellike materials. Velcro dots with adhesive backs can be attached to flannel characters. Velcro dots or snaps can also be sewn to material and be used to attach costumes or other decorations to characters.

Pellon

Purchase Pellon fabric interfacing at your local fabric or craft store. Pellon, while not quite as sticky as flannel, acts much the same when placed on a flannel board. Pellon is a very thin, white material that is easily colored with marking pens. Pellon can be cut easily with a scissors into just about any shape. Try this material as an alternative to flannel or felt when you want to have a highly decorated, colorful cut-out character.

Paper Cut-Outs with Masking Tape

Use construction paper or cardboard (tagboard or railroad board) to make cut-out characters, scenery, etc. Put a few pieces of rolled up masking tape on the back of the cut-outs so that they will stick to your display board. Before you put the masking tape on the cardboard or construction paper, attach a couple pieces of cellophane tape to the back of the cut-out. Place your masking tape over the cellophane tape so that when you pull the masking tape off, it will not tear. You can save cardboard or construction cut-outs for years with a little care.

The Most Common High-Tech Teaching Tools

The most commonly used high-tech teaching tools are ...

NINE

The Overhead Projector and Transparencies

Next to the chalkboard, the overhead projector is probably the single most useful audio-visual tool that a teacher can use. The overhead can be used as an electronic chalkboard, a silhouette puppet theater, a light source for a shadow play, and a device for making picture enlargements. The overhead projector also can be used in a lighted room and allows the teacher to face the class while teaching. Overheads have the added benefit of being easy for students to use.

Transparencies are also easy to use and can be made by hand, photocopier, or Thermo-Fax machine. They can be colored by using marking pens or special colored adhesives. Transparencies of Bible maps and other specialized content can be purchased through your religious book store. Blackline masters, which are often provided with teachers materials, can also be used to create transparencies.

When you put the transparency on the projector, remember that what you see is what you get. As you look at the overhead's stage (the glass plate through which light shines), whatever you see on the stage is what is being projected on the screen. If you "read" your transparency correctly as it sits on the stage, it will read correctly on the screen behind you. The only time you should reverse your transparency is when you rear project on a screen in front of the overhead.

Making Overhead Transparencies

The overhead projector is ideal for making enlargements of maps, letters, and other pictures. Here are several uses.

1. Bulletin board letters.

Below are some examples that you can enlarge onto posterboard or construction paper by using the overhead projector and a transparency made from a copy of the letters.

ABC123
FATHER

Jesus

Several full sets of letters and numerals are provided in Appendix B. Make several cut-out copies of each set of letters because you will need multiple letters to spell out words for your bulletin boards. Here's how to do it.

a. Make a photocopy of the pages of letters.

b. Make a transparency with a Thermo-Fax machine or use a photocopy of a transparency directly from the copier.

c. Project the transparency onto your posterboard or construction paper

d. Move the overhead toward or away from the wall as you project. As you move the overhead toward the wall, the projection will become smaller (you will have to keep refocusing the projector as you move it into different positions). As you move the projector away from the wall, the projection will become larger.

e. When you get your projection to the desired size, bring it into sharp focus and then trace your enlarged letters on the posterboard.

f. Cut out the letters for display.

2. Tracing on a transparency to make an enlargement.

If you find a map or a simple illustration that you would like to enlarge, you can trace the outline on a clear transparency, project it, and then copy it on other material.

3. Creating your own images.

There are several basic ways to create your own images on transparencies:

a. Use either permanent or washable colored marking pens on a clear transparency.

b. Create a permanent outline image by drawing a blackline image with a soft (preferably a no. 1) lead pencil on a white sheet of paper. Then make the transparency either by photocopying or the Thermo-Fax process.

c. Make a color transparency by a color copier process (very expensive) or a color-lift process (much less expensive). Color lifts can be made using two processes. The first uses clear adhesive shelf paper; the second is done with a laminating machine.

I. Adhesive-paper Process.

Buy a roll of clear adhesive shelf paper.

a. Select a picture that you would like to make into a transparency from a magazine that uses clay-coated paper (i.e. Newsweek, Time, U.S. News and World Report, Sports Illustrated). National Geographic and newspapers will not work well for color lifts. The thin slick finished paper used in the types of magazines listed will give you the best results.

b. Cut a piece of adhesive paper to match the size of the picture you want to lift.

c. Peel back about a quarter inch edge of the backing paper from the adhesive paper and stick it to your table. Then place your picture face up under the adhesive paper. Peel the rest of the backing paper from the adhesive and carefully smooth it onto the picture. You can use a squeegee or a hand roller to get rid of most of the air bubbles. Then take a spoon and thoroughly rub all the air bubbles out.

d. Place the adhesive sheet into cool water and allow it to soak for a few minutes.

e. Gently rub the paper off the adhesive paper. The ink will adhere to the adhesive sheet and the paper will fall away. You will have transferred (lifted) the ink to the plastic. When the transparency is dry, you may wish to spray the tacky side of the transparency with a clear plastic spray (from hardware or paint store) to preserve it.

II. Laminator Process. (Using a laminator to produce a color-lift transparency.)

A laminator is used to preserve flat materials (maps, posters, pictures, cut-outs, etc.) by encapsulating them between two sheets of transparent film. Next to a color photocopy transparency, the color-lift transparency produced with a laminator gives the best results. Laminators can be found at your local school district's media center or at business stores specializing in copying and binding materials. Here's how to make a color-lift transparency with a laminator.

a. Select a picture from a glossy magazine such as *Time, Newsweek, U.S. News,* etc. (Note: These magazines use a clay-coated paper that allows the ink to be lifted from the paper with ease. Not all magazine papers will give you a good result. You will need to experiment a little.)

b. Place it face up on a sheet of white paper (which will serve as a backing sheet).

c. Send both the picture and the white backing sheet of paper through the laminator together.

d. Cut the picture and white backing sheet out of the laminate leaving about a half-inch of laminate around the border.

e. Send the laminated picture and backing sheet though the laminator again. (This will give strength to your transparency and make it easier to work with after you have soaked the paper off.)

f. Trim the picture from the laminate with a scissors or utility knife. The white paper backing sheet will be removed leaving only one side of your picture with laminate.

g. Soak your one-sided laminated picture in cool water for a few minutes. The paper should come off with relative ease. Sometimes you will have to rub the paper residue off with your thumb or with a sponge to get it thoroughly clean.

h. When the transparency is completely dry, you may wish to send it through the laminator one more time. This will stiffen the transparency and make it even more transparent. Be careful when you send it through the laminator. If you send it through unevenly, you will get unwanted wrinkles in the transparency. Try an experiment or two to get the hang of it.

4. Using an overhead transparency roll attachment.

You can purchase overhead transparency projection rolls made of heavy-duty plastic. These transparency rolls can be easily attached to your overhead projector. You can draw on these rolls with washable transparency pens or grease pencils. You can illustrate an entire story and then roll it across the projector as you retell it. When you're finished, erase the story and you're ready for another. By putting your information on a transparency roll, you can quickly roll from one picture to the next. The rolls come in various lengths from 25 to 50 feet in length. You can put a lot of information on these transparency rolls for a reasonable cost.

5. Framing a transparency.

It is always a good practice to put your transparencies into a cardboard frame. Cardboard frames can be purchased from local audio-visual suppliers. A frame helps out in three ways: a) it makes the transparency easier to handle, b) it allows you to write important information on the frame for easy reference (this eliminates the use of 3″ × 5″ cards and other notes that seem to get lost in the shuffle), c) the frame makes it possible for you to use overlays and other revealing techniques.

Use masking tape to mount your transparency to the cardboard frame.

Write notes to yourself on the frame and number your transparencies for easy reference.

Add overlays to your transparencies by taping other transparencies to the cardboard frame.

Tape sheets of paper to the cardboard frame and reveal segments of the transparencies at different times.

Using Computer Printers

Computers and laser printers have become more commonplace in our schools, offices, churches, and homes. Using word-processing programs to generate transparencies is probably the most efficient method for making transparencies. There are also more sophisticated drawing programs available to help create illustrations. A laser printer makes the cleanest copy for projection, but a dot-matrix printer can produce a good image as well. I usually make a photocopy of a dot-matrix printout before making a Thermo-Fax transparency. The photocopy darkens in the dots and makes the transparency sharper. You can also adjust the temperature control on your Thermo-Fax to darken the transparency slightly when using a dot-matrix printout.

General Tips and Rules of Thumb for Use

Avoid looking back at the screen when you are projecting. Once you have focused your transparency, you need not constantly look back at the screen. Keep your eyes on the class.

If you need to point out something on the transparency, point directly on the transparency using a pencil or a pen (your index finger will also do in a pinch). Avoid pointing at the screen with your hand.

Make sure your lettering is large enough to be seen easily. There are two general rules of thumb for lettering transparencies:

1. The Eight-Foot Rule: After making your transparency, put it eight feet away from you. If you can read the lettering easily it is probably okay to project.

2. The Six-by-Six Rule: In general, there should be no more than six words per line and no more than six lines per transparency.

Like any rules of thumb, these rules can be bent and broken. What's most important is that your transparencies be clear and easy to read. When in doubt, err on the side of clarity and simplicity. Don't try to cram too much information on any one transparency.

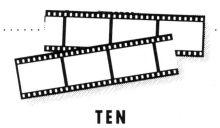

TEN

Making Slides without a Camera

Even if you don't have a camera, you and your students can have a great time telling stories by making 35mm slides. Here are some suggestions:

Purchased Slide Blanks

The Eastman Kodak company makes a product called "Kodak Ecktagraphic Write-on Slides" that you can get from your local office supply store or from Highsmith Corporation. (Call 1–800–558–2110.)

Write-on slides are made with a translucent material that can be written on with ink, colored marking pens, ballpoint pens (any color), and pencils (any color). You will notice that the slide's cardboard mount is labeled "Write on this side." The side that you write on has a dull finish to which ink and pencil will adhere. If you try to write on the glossy side of the slide, you will not have much luck. Since the slides are clearly labeled, you will have no difficulty in figuring out which is the correct side on which to write.

The pictures you draw will be very small (1⁵⁄₁₆ × ⅞). When projected, however, the pictures will be very large. Because the drawings will be small, it is best to keep each very simple. Stick figures and simple shapes work well. Try to draw only one segment of the story per slide. Here is an example of how one could tell the story of Noah and the Ark using write-on slides.

Script

1. "Noah and the Ark"

2. God said to Noah, "Build an Ark." Noah listens.

3. Noah's sons, Shem, Ham, and Japheth, help him build the ark.

4. Evil people mock Noah.

5. The ark is one-quarter finished.

6. The ark is half-finished.

7. The ark is finished.

8. Noah gathers up two of every kind of animal—

9. Two turtles,

10. Two bears,

11. Two birds,

12. Two giraffes,

13. Two rabbits,

14. Two hippos,

15. Two snakes,

16. Two horses, and

17. Two pigs.

(The number of animals will vary according to number of children in the class and the number of slides assigned to each member of the class).

18. The rains came. The ark floats on the water for

19. Forty days and nights.

20. Noah sends out a raven to see if the land is dry.

21. Raven comes back without anything in its beak.

22. Noah sends out a dove to see if anything is growing yet.

23. Dove comes back with a branch in its beak.

24. Finally, the waters go away, leaving the ark on the mountains of Ararat.

25. On land, Noah builds an altar to praise God.

26. God sends a rainbow to show that he would never send a flood again.

(As many slides as you want of rainbows.)

27. The End

Homemade Slides

Another way to make your own 35mm slides is to draw on transparency film and mount the transparencies in 35mm slide mounts. Slide mounts are the 2″ × 2″ cardboard frames into which you will place (mount) your transparencies for projection. The slide mounts come in a variety of sizes (half-frame, Instamatic 126, full-frame, and super). For our purposes the full frame or super slide mounts are the most practical. Transparency slides can be made in the following ways:

Drawing Method

1. Make photocopies or spirit duplicator copies of the grid found in Appendix C.

2. Place a clear piece of acetate or write-on transparency film on top of the grid and draw your picture(s).

3. Carefully cut out the transparency picture(s) according to the guide dots.

4. Place transparency into the centering frame of the slide mount.

5. Fold the slide mount together and iron the edges with a tacking iron or a hand iron (low or synthetic heat). There is a heat sensitive adhesive that will seal the edges of the slide. Be careful not to touch the iron to the transparency surface.

6. Put the slide on the table so that it reads correctly as it faces you.

7. Make a thumb-spot on the lower left hand edge of the cardboard slide mount. You can simply draw a dot, or you can make a nice round dot with a stamp pad and pencil eraser. The thumb-spot is used to help you make sure that your slide is correctly positioned in the slide tray.

Pick up the slide in your right hand, holding your thumb over the thumb-spot. Place the slide in the tray so that it is upside down, with the thumb-spot now positioned in the upper right hand corner as it sits in the tray. If your thumb-spotting is done correctly, your slides will always project properly.

Color Lift Adhesive Paper Method

Color-lift slides are made by the same process described in the last chapter. The only difference is that you will mount the transparency in a 35mm slide mount for projection in a slide projector.

1. Use the slide mount's window to find pictures (on clay-coated paper) that you want to project.

2. When you have positioned your picture in the slide window, use a pen to trace around the outer edge of the slide mount.

3. Cut out a two-inch square piece of adhesive paper, peel off the backing paper, adhere the paper to the picture, and rub out all the air bubbles with a spoon, a butter knife handle, or scissors handle. Rub the surface of the film in horizontal, vertical, and diagonal ways to assure the best adhesion.

4. Cut the paper away from the adhesive paper.

5. Soak the picture in cool water.

6. Gently rub off the paper from the adhesive.

7. Cut out the picture so that it fits into the centering frame of the slide mount.

8. Seal the slide mount with an iron and thumb-spot on the cardboard edge of the slide mount as described above.

Color-Lift Laminator Method

You can also make slides using a laminator (see page 115). The process is the same as described in the last chapter, only this time the transparencies will be mounted in slide mounts. You can also do many laminated slides at one time.

1. Place all pictures on a piece of plain white paper.

2. Run them through the laminator twice.

3. Cut out the pictures.

4. Place the pictures in cool water for a few minutes.

5. Peel away the paper from the transparency and wash thoroughly. (Use a sponge, or lightly rub the residue away with your fingers.)

6. Cut to fit the slide mount.

7. Seal slide mount with iron and thumb-spot.

Typewriter Method with Thermo-Fax or Photocopy Transparencies

Type directly onto a copy of the slide grid sheet (Appendix C). If you are using a carbon ribbon, you may make a Thermo-Fax copy of the grid sheet and then proceed to cut out and mount your slides as described before. You can also use photocopy transparencies to do the same thing.

Computer-Generated Slides from the Laser Printer

Many people have access to a computer and a high-quality printer. You can easily produce high quality typing on slides by using a computer and laser printer. If you type within the $7/8 \times 1 5/16$ window of the 35mm slide, you can project almost any kind of text you want. Here are a few examples:

Hymn texts can be projected (less expensive and less wasteful than printing out copies for a large group).

> *Note: Hymns in public domain may be reproduced in this manner, however, you must seek permission for the use of copyrighted hymns or other texts before you reproduce them in any manner.*

Memory texts can be projected. Words can also be left out of the text for the children to fill in by speaking/reading as the text is projected. The first slide can have the text without key words and the second can correctly state the complete passage. Highlight the previously missing words with a colored marking pens or in italics for emphasis.

Slide 1:

I was _____ when
they said unto me,
"Let us go into the
_____ of the _____."
Psalm 122:1

As you fill your slide tray with different hymns or texts for projection, you can label the outside rim of the tray. For easy reference, use adhesive labels to indicate the positions of the hymns or texts.

ELEVEN

Photography and Video

Here are some reasons why every teacher should keep a camera within reach.

Photographs and slides ...

> are excellent instructional tools;
>
> are great tools for public relations and communication;
>
> allow you to keep a visual record of what children do in the class room;
>
> help to build relationships between students and teachers and parents;
>
> stimulate student interest;
>
> help to generate classroom discussion;
>
> help students to remember content of lessons;
>
> are useful helps in worship;
>
> are easy to make;
>
> are relatively inexpensive;
>
> can be easily stored and saved for future use;
>
> help us to tell our own story.

We all know the saying that "a picture is worth a thousand words." Well, it's true. Pictures can help us to quickly remember events, ideas, concepts, and facts. They can explain a difficult concept when words only get in the way. Pictures and slides can also help stimulate students to express their ideas in both spoken and written ways. Visual images are so important for student learning that I believe that every teacher should know how to use a camera.

Which Camera?

Many people feel very threatened by cameras. My wife, for example, hates to take pictures with my "complex" camera. As a result, I have almost no pictures of myself standing in front of the Colosseum in Rome or the Cathedral of Notre Dame de Paris. Try as I might, I have been unsuccessful in trying to teach my wife how to focus my camera. If you are like my wife, you need not despair; there *is* a camera built just for you.

Last year my wife and I took a short vacation. We had been on the road for about an hour when I realized I had forgotten to bring my camera. When we stopped for lunch, we found a little discount department store next to the restaurant. To my surprise I found an inexpensive Kodak Star 25 camera that came with batteries, film, and some coupons for the purchase of film. The camera had a built-in flash and a sliding lens cap designed to keep the lens from being scratched. We (and I emphasize we) used the camera throughout the trip. When we got home and had the pictures developed, we were very pleased with the results. Every picture (including the ones we took inside a cave we explored) turned out perfectly. My wife successfully took pictures of me as I stood in front of various landmarks. The camera, about $25, was one of the best investments I have ever made. I was so pleased with the camera that I bought another one just like it. I keep one at home and one in my office at school. I'm ready to get a picture at a moment's notice.

Moral: You don't need to spend lots of money or have any expertise to get a good picture. (However, if you still have camera-phobia, find someone at your church who is a camera fanatic and enlist his or her services for the more complex shots.)

Typical Cameras

1. Simple point-and-shoot, instant-type cameras (always look for built-in flash). These cameras usually take 126 or 35mm film. Found at discount and drug stores.

2. Polaroid instant cameras—great when you want results right away! Also found at discount and drug stores.

3. 35mm range-finder cameras. Found at department and discount stores. You will have to learn how to focus and set the light meter. Not too difficult to use, but not as easy to use when taking close-up shots.

4. Single-lens reflex cameras (SLR). More sophisticated, but the most flexible camera for our purposes. A little more expensive than range-finder cameras, but lens can easily be interchanged for telephoto (long range) and close-up shots. If you feel intimidated by this camera, make sure you find that photo fanatic to help you out. The photo fanatic will own one or more of these cameras and will be happy to help you do what needs to be done.

Some Ideas on Using Photographs

1. Take pictures of each member of your class and display them on a bulletin board in your classroom. Use adhesive labels to put each student's name on the picture.

2. During a home visit, take a picture of the child with the parents. Display these on a bulletin board, make a Sunday school family album, send the picture home with the children at the end of the year as a memento.

3. Take a picture of the child(ren) in the Sunday school or vacation Bible school class and send it to the parents.

4. Take a close-up picture of each child's face by getting as close as you can

to the child with your camera. If you are using a simple camera or a Polaroid camera, you should probably not be closer than four or five feet. Have duplicate set(s) of pictures developed at your photo store. When the pictures are developed, you will have one for display on your bulletin board and others to use for various purposes.

a. For younger children: Cut out the face of the child and glue it to a tongue depressor (available from craft supply stores). Paint stick (get them free from your paint store) or Popsicle stick. Label the stick with the child's name. Put the "sticks with pics" in a coffee can labeled "Mrs. Smith's 4th-Grade Class." Have another can labeled "I am here today" sitting next to the other can. When children come to class, they can take their "stick with pic" out of one can and put it into the other for attendance purposes.

b. Make a collage of Sunday school or vacation Bible school faces.

c. Have children draw pictures of themselves using their picture where their face would be.

5. Send a picture of your class to your local newspaper. This is especially important when your Sunday school or vacation Bible school is putting on a play, doing some community service, or when you are advertising your program of Christian education.

6. Take pictures of your activities throughout the year using slide film. At the end of the year have an open house and show the slides to parents and children.

7. Include slides of the year's activities in a worship service that celebrates Christian education.

8. Bring an album of pictures from last year's class to show parents when you make a home visit.

9. Show slides of Sunday school and VBS activities to new congregation members or potential members.

10. Take photos or slides of student projects and keep them as examples to show next year's students what has been done in the past.

11. Take close-up slides of pictures that students have drawn and use them to tell the story in church or Sunday school. Here's how to do it.

A few years ago one of my former students asked me if I could help her do some photography for her church's Christmas service. She had her class do illustrations of the Christmas story and wanted me to take slides of the artwork that could be projected during the service. I used a 35mm single-lens reflex camera with a macro (close-up) lens and a special camera stand with lights to do the photography. The set up looks like this.

With a macro lens or other less-expensive close-up lens and a copy stand you can easily make high-quality slide duplications of pictures. If you have access to this kind of equipment or if someone in your congregation owns this equipment, you are in good shape. Equipment like

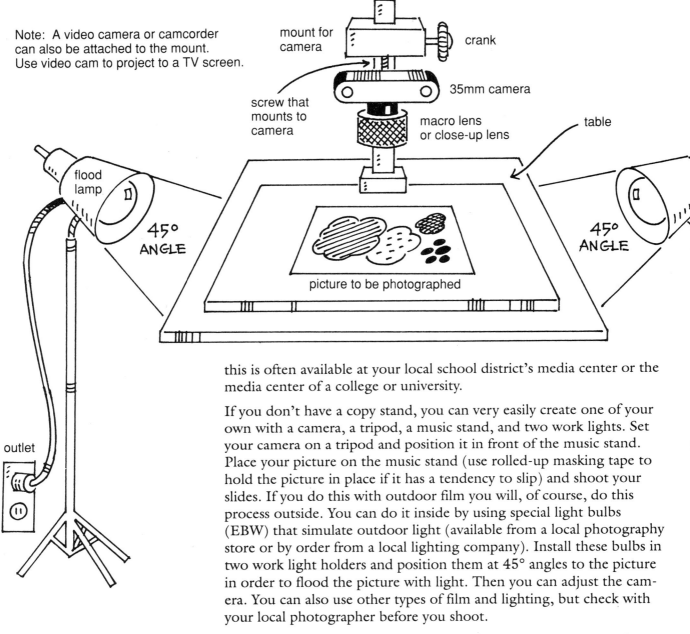

Note: A video camera or camcorder can also be attached to the mount. Use video cam to project to a TV screen.

mount for camera

crank

screw that mounts to camera

35mm camera

macro lens or close-up lens

table

flood lamp

45° ANGLE

45° ANGLE

picture to be photographed

outlet

this is often available at your local school district's media center or the media center of a college or university.

If you don't have a copy stand, you can very easily create one of your own with a camera, a tripod, a music stand, and two work lights. Set your camera on a tripod and position it in front of the music stand. Place your picture on the music stand (use rolled-up masking tape to hold the picture in place if it has a tendency to slip) and shoot your slides. If you do this with outdoor film you will, of course, do this process outside. You can do it inside by using special light bulbs (EBW) that simulate outdoor light (available from a local photography store or by order from a local lighting company). Install these bulbs in two work light holders and position them at 45° angles to the picture in order to flood the picture with light. Then you can adjust the camera. You can also use other types of film and lighting, but check with your local photographer before you shoot.

12. Pictures of students posing different scenes from Bible stories or hymn stanzas. Have children dress in Old/New Testament clothes (old bathrobes or bedsheet togas). Pictures of various scenes can be posed and photographed. A narration that accompanies the slides is very effective for telling the story in words and pictures. You might do the Christmas story, the story of the Wise Men, Abraham and Isaac, Jesus and the 10 lepers, and the Sermon on the Mount in this way.

You can also illustrate stanzas of hymns in this way. The story of "Doubting Thomas" as told in the hymn "Ye Sons and Daughters of the King" lends itself to a photo/slide presentation. These could, of course, also be told using student illustrations, as was suggested in number 11.

13. Write a story and illustrate it with photographs taken of and/or by the children.

14. Do a photo story using puppets as characters. Here you could simply take flash photos or slides of the puppet theater and puppets as you do the puppet drama. Add live narration as the slides are shown or record the story on an audiocassette tape to be played along with the slides. Hint: If you are making an audiocassette recording that you want to play along with your slides, an easy way to signal a slide change is to make an audible beep on the tape. You can do this by using a water glass and a pencil. Whenever you wish to signal that the next slide should be shown, lightly strike an empty water glass with a pencil as you make your recording. You will get a ping sound on the tape that will signal the projectionist when to advance to the next slide.

Using Video

Video tape recording is the fastest growing technology for popular consumption next to the personal computer. If your congregation doesn't own a VHS camcorder, there's bound to be someone in your congregation that does. Video recording, like photography, is easy to learn and can enhance student participation, interest, and learning.

The camcorder can be used very much like a 35mm camera to capture images on tape. These images can then be shown on a television screen or projected by using a video projector.

Video projectors are becoming more popular in schools and churches, but you will probably be viewing your videos on a TV screen. When you use a TV, try to use the largest size screen possible and seat your audience in a semicircle around the television. When showing videos to younger children, it is important to try to get the TV low enough so they won't be craning their necks too much in order to see the screen. I use a rule of thumb that says for every diagonal inch of TV screen, one person may view. In other words, with a 13″ diagonal screen, no more than 13 people (in a semicircle). For a 25″ diagonal screen, 25 people. Remember, though, this is just a rule of thumb. Remain flexible.

Some Ways to Use Video to Tell the Story

1. Video tape any performance-type activity. If the upper grade children do a skit, puppet drama, or pantomime, video tape it and show it to the younger children. If the children do a Gospeldrama in church, video tape it and keep it in your video library for replay at a later date or when your lesson calls for it.

2. Keep a video library of important events in the life of your church, Sunday school, or VBS programs. You can edit these for a video "yearbook," or show them to new or potential members.

3. If you have a picture in a book that is too small to be seen by the entire class, view the picture on a TV screen by zooming in on the picture with the close up lens of the camcorder. (Most camcorders today come equipped with a macro lens for super close-up shots.) Put the picture or

book or map on a music stand and aim the camera at the picture that you want the class to see. The TV will show an enlarged picture of the image you are shooting.

4. You can also read stories by using the same method. If you want the class to easily view the pictures of the story without having to slow pan the book in front of their faces, use the camcorder to show the pictures of the book on the TV screen.

5. Have the children create their own video productions. For example:

a. Do a video interview with the pastor, the president of the congregation, other teachers, the board of elders, etc.

b. Interview a biblical character such as Moses, St. Paul, David, Shadrach, Meshach, Abednego, or King Saul.

c. Use a "Tonight Show" format to discuss an event or theme from the Bible. The show could feature musical and dramatic talent as well as interviews.

d. Do a "Weather Report from the Holy Land Show" using maps of the Holy Land. This is a good way to teach Bible geography.

e. Have members of the high school class tape a church service and take it to the home of a shut-in or a person in the hospital.

f. Video tape a service from another church and view it during class time. Compare and contrast the ways other people worship.

g. Tape and interview a person or persons of a different denomination or faith. View the interviews in class and discuss the differences and similarities between denominations and faiths.

h. Have members of the class put together a documentary. Some issues for consideration might be: A Christian comments on war (interview people who have served in the military during wartime and ask them what role their faith played in getting them through that time of their life); A Christian reacts to death (interview people who have had to face the death of a loved one); A Christian talks about racism (or social injustice, abortion, politics, ethics in business, evangelism going away to college, getting married, etc.).

i. As another type of documentary, follow the students as they do a service project in the community or for a particular person in the congregation. Video documentation of a visit to a nursing home or a hospital is an excellent way to have the children share their experiences with others. As students gain this kind of experience at telling their own stories to people in the congregation, they become better equipped to share their faith stories with their friends and neighbors who may not be members of the church.

j. Do some "commercials" that "sell" or teach an idea, a memory verse, or a catechism passage. You can also do a commercial that introduces a Bible story. For example:

"Greetings TV viewers! Today's Bible story is brought to you by the first

eight books of the Old Testament. That's right, Genesis, Exodus, Leviticus, Numbers, Deuteronomy, Joshua, Judges, and Ruth. ... That's right. And all these books can be found right here (*hold up a Bible*) in the front part of the Bible. Remember those books? Well, let's see if you do. I'll say the first book and then you say the other seven books in their correct order. Okay, here we go. Genesis (*pause*) ... did you say Exodus? Well, you got it right on the first try! What comes after Exodus (*pause*) ... right again—Leviticus—you're doing great. What comes after Leviticus? Correct-a-mundo! It's the book of Numbers! It's tough to fool you. Okay, the next book starts with the letter 'D' for (*pause*) ... you got it—Deuteronomy. Only three more to go. Can you say them all in a row? Well, what do you know about that; I made a rhyme! All right, lets hear 'em. Right again: Joshua, Judges, and—last but not least—Ruth. Tomorrow our show will be brought to you by the Old Testament books from First Samuel through Psalms. And now, back to our story for today: Daniel in the Lions Den. By the way, in what book of the Bible is the story of Daniel in the Lion's Den found? Did you say Daniel? Then you are correct! I bet you thought that was a trick question, didn't you? That's right, it's the book of Daniel, the sixth chapter to be exact. And now for our story."

Use Video to Watch Yourself

Tape record yourself as you teach a lesson or tell a Bible story. Nothing will help you to do a better job of teaching than watching yourself teach. Here are some important things to remember:

1. You'll be motivated. Knowing that you are going to tape yourself, you will probably work just a bit harder during your preparation time. Nothing spiffs up a lesson like knowing you are going to be observing yourself.

2. Don't let the camera scare you. Set it and forget it. In a few minutes you will be teaching as if it weren't there. You will get a pretty honest view of how you teach by the end of the session.

3. Don't be too hard on yourself. Remember the first time that you heard your voice on a tape recorder? You probably said, "That doesn't sound like me!" Everyone else who heard the tape said that it sounded just like you, but you thought that the sound wasn't correct. The same thing happens when you first view yourself on video tape. You think to yourself, "That can't be me!" It will be you, but don't look at what you perceive only as your negatives. All too often we tend to dwell on what we think we didn't accomplish. Remember to look for all the positive things that happen during the lesson.

4. Look at the tape with a friend or an experienced teacher. He or she will be able to point out all the things you are doing right. There is always room for improvement, of course. That's why you're taping yourself—to find out both what's right about your teaching and where you can improve. A friend or experienced teacher will help to temper your criticism of yourself.

5. Choose a lesson to videotape that you are confident about. Don't videotape yourself on a lesson that you think is going to be problematic. Give yourself your best shot.

6. Videotape yourself at least once or twice a year. I try to videotape myself several times a month, but I'm teaching almost every day. Whenever I see myself, I am reminded about how much I have to do, and how far I have come. Whenever I see myself, I come away with ideas of how I might improve my teaching.

The reason for doing this is simple. The children we teach deserve the very best instruction that we can provide. By observing ourselves through video tape, we avail ourselves of the most accurate view of how and what we are doing in the classroom. This is not something to be afraid of. It is an opportunity for us to grow and improve our abilities to communicate the faith with the students whom God has placed before us.

Remember: You're Not Alone

It's important to remember that where your experience and expertise ends, someone else's begins. Never hesitate to ask someone for help with photography or videography. If you know photographer and videographer people in your community, you will be able to do almost any kind of visual image production that you want to do. Make a list of the people you know in your congregation who know something about photography or video. Then call them up and ask them what kind of equipment they have and if they would, sometime in the future, give you a hand at producing some pictures or videos with your class. I'm certain that they will be happy to help.

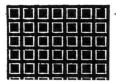

TWELVE

Electronic Game Boards

Electronic game boards—matching items in place to those in another—are great ways to encourage memory work, teach factual material, and help students test themselves. The concept can also be used to create exciting bulletin boards and posters.

After making the board and attaching the two lists (or a list and a map, or ...), use a Continuity Tester (a wire gizmo with a battery and small light bulb) to touch two places on the board. If the match is correct, the bulb lights up. Simple.

Possibility for matches are almost endless. Here are just a few:

1. Match the books of the Bible with the stories found in the books.
   Genesis—Adam and Eve, Abraham and Isaac, Joseph and his brothers
   1 Samuel—Eli, Saul, and David
   Exodus—Moses is Born, Plagues of Egypt, the Passover
   Daniel—Three Men in a Fiery Furnace, Nebuchadnezzar's Dream
   Etc.

2. Match Bible passages with biblical reference:
   God so loved the world—John 3:16
   The Lord is my shepherd—Psalm 23
   Let there be light—Genesis 1:3
   Take off your sandals for the place ... is holy ground—Exodus 3:5
   Etc.

3. Match place names to their locations on the map of the Holy Land:
   Jerusalem, Dead Sea, Sea of Galilee, Jordan River, Bethlehem, Jericho, Tyre, Sidon, Damascus, Mt. Carmel, etc.

4. Match the number of the commandment with the correct commandment.

5. Leave words out of memory verses and have the children match the correct word that goes in the blank to the correct passage.

I'll give you some examples of generic electric boards. Once you understand the basic idea behind their design, you will be able to come up with lots of different ideas on how to make and use them.

Construction of an Electric Game Board

Cardboard and Aluminum Foil (easiest and least expensive to make)

Step 1

Assemble these materials:

1. Scissors or sharp utility knife

2. A continuity tester. This simple circuit tester, purchased at a hardware store, consists of a battery, a light bulb, a small metal probe, and a wire with an alligator clip on the end. Cost: about $5.00–$7.00. You can also make one of your own; ask the hardware store person for the parts.

3. A hand-held hole punch

4. Pens, marking pens, pencils, etc.

5. Glue stick (optional)

6. Masking or cellophane tape

7. Poster board or cardboard

8. A roll of aluminum foil (heavy duty is best, but not necessary)

Step 2

Make a list of 8–10 items that you want students to match.

Step 3

Punch the necessary number of holes on each side of a piece of cardboard.

Step 4

Write your items to be matched next to each hole in the cardboard.

Step 5

On the back of the cardboard, designate which holes on one side match with the holes on the other side. This will save you time as you match and connect your aluminum foil "wires" later on.

Step 6

Put several long strips of cellophane tape on a sheet of aluminum foil (this will give the foil added strength and keep it from tearing as you work with it). The strips should be long so that you can cut them to size later.

Step 7

Cut aluminum foil strips and attach them to the back of the cardboard so that the aluminum foil (untaped side) is over the matching holes for each of the items to be matched. Use small pieces of tape to hold the aluminum strip in place over the holes.

Once you have the strip placed correctly, tape over the entire length of the strip with a piece of masking or cellophane tape. (You don't want any accidental short circuits between your aluminum tape strips.) To make sure that you have done it correctly, use your continuity tester to see that it lights up when you connect it to the holes.

Repeat this process until all holes are matched with the aluminum foil "wires."

Step 8

Do a final check to make sure all circuits are correct and that there are no short circuits.

Step 9

Cover the back of your board with another piece of cardboard to hide the circuits and protect them from being damaged.

Step 10

Use in class.

Electronic Game Board

Front side

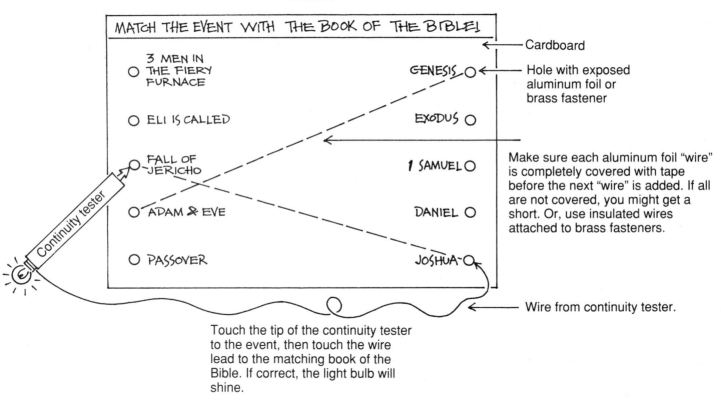

MATCH THE EVENT WITH THE BOOK OF THE BIBLE!

3 MEN IN THE FIERY FURNACE

ELI IS CALLED

FALL OF JERICHO

ADAM & EVE

PASSOVER

GENESIS

EXODUS

1 SAMUEL

DANIEL

JOSHUA

Continuity tester

— Cardboard

— Hole with exposed aluminum foil or brass fastener

Make sure each aluminum foil "wire" is completely covered with tape before the next "wire" is added. If all are not covered, you might get a short. Or, use insulated wires attached to brass fasteners.

— Wire from continuity tester.

Touch the tip of the continuity tester to the event, then touch the wire lead to the matching book of the Bible. If correct, the light bulb will shine.

Variation 1: Use Brass Fasteners instead of Holes

Instead of punching holes, use brass fasteners. Make a small incision with the tip of utility knife and push the brass fasteners through the cardboard; then open its wings. Tape the aluminum foil strip (untaped side) firmly to the brass fastener wings. Brass fasteners allow you a little more flexibility of placement since the hole punch usually can't reach everywhere on the cardboard. Or, use holes on one side of the cardboard and brass fasteners in places where a hole punch can't reach. Here's an example of a map game board that uses a hole punch and brass fasteners.

Variation 2: Use Real Wire with the Brass Fasteners

Using very thin (cheap) stranded wire, strip about an inch of insulation away from the ends of the wire. Wrap the wire tightly around the wings of the brass fasteners and tape the wire firmly to the fastener. If you have a soldering pencil or gun, use that for a better connection.

Variation 3: Use a Box and Alligator Clip Wires

The advantage of a box is that you can easily change your circuits and hide the connections from the user. The advantage of the alligator clip wires is how easy they are to change for a new game.

Go to your local electronic parts store and buy alligator clip wires. These thin wires come in a variety of lengths and thicknesses. Each end of the wire has a small alligator clip that you can clip to the wings of a brass fastener. If your wires are too short to reach between two fasteners, you can clip two or three wires together. The little teeth of the alligator clips hold quite well, but you may wish to put a small piece of masking tape around the clips to insure that they won't come apart by accident.

Use the top of a box to make your game board. Attach the alligator clips and put the top on the box. If you want to change the matching categories or change the circuits, all you have to do is remove the box top and reconnect the alligator clip wires to correspond with the new matching questions.

Variation 4: Heavy-Duty Board

If you want to make a heavy-duty, all-purpose electronic board in which matching information and circuits can easily be changed, use plywood or masonite and screws and nuts. You will need:

1. A ¼ piece of plywood or Masonite board (size determined by need)

2. A box of ¾ round-head screws, with nuts sized to fit the screws (two per screw)

3. Wire (inexpensive bell wire works well) or alligator clip wires

4. A screwdriver

5. A small wrench

6. Power drill (optional)

Screw a line of screws on both sides of the board. Put one nut on each screw from the back side of the board and tighten it. Put a second nut on each screw, but do not tighten fully.

Put your matching questions on the front of the game board (you can use sticky notes or tape cards with the matching items to the board). Connect the wires to the screws by tightening the second nut down on the wire. You can, of course, use alligator clips if you wish.

THIRTEEN

Using Songs to Teach the Faith

One of the most important resources that we have for teaching the faith is the hymnal. It contains not only the great music and poetry of the church throughout the ages but also holds a wealth of material to help us teach the faith. Hymnals contain important dates in the church year, the propers for each day of the church year, prayers for many occasions, liturgies of the church, special services and rites, devotional reading suggestions, the catechism, psalms, chants and canticles for the church year, various indexes which give information on the authors of hymn texts and composers of hymn tunes, copyright information, listings such as the Hymn of the Day, topical indexes (hymns which are especially appropriate for particular celebrations), hymn tune lists (the name of hymn *tune* often differs from the hymn's common name, which is usually based on the first line of the hymn's text), and metrical listings of each hymn (useful if you want to sing a hymn text to various tunes).

We all use the hymnal at least once a week when we go to church, but we could use it every day. The hymnal is a great gift to the church, but it is sometimes taken for granted. The hymnal is an endless source of devotional material if we take the time to explore its depths.

A few years ago I decided to systematically go through my hymnal by reading, singing, and playing everything between its covers. I saw the hymnal in a new way. I found hymns that were old friends and made new friends as well. I rediscovered that the hymnal is more than just a book of songs; it is a biblical history book, a "lives of the saints" book, a religious poetry book, a Bible commentary, a catechism, a church history text, and a devotional guide for every day of the year.

As teachers of the faith, we need to explore this great resource. The hymnal puts us in touch with men and women of the faith who have written texts and tunes to the glory of God. It brings us into contact with saints throughout the ages who share their reflections, testimony, and strength of faith with us as we sing their words and music. As we listen to their words, accompanied by music composed to amplify the text, we learn about what it means to be faithful.

Here are some suggestions regarding the use of the hymnal for teaching the faith.

Take Time in Class to Reflect and Explain

Set aside a few minutes each class period to reflect on the hymn that you have chosen to sing for your opening or closing devotion. Look at the vocabulary of the hymn. Decide how you will explain what a particular phrase of the text means.

Here are some phrases from hymns which students may wonder about.[1] Can you explain their meaning and origin?

1. From "Hark, the Voice of Jesus Calling"(*LW* 318): "You can be like faithful Aaron, Holding up the prophet's hands" (stanza 3) and "Here am I. Send me, send me!" (stanza 4).

2. From "How Firm a Foundation"(*LW* 411): "The flames will not hurt you, I only design Your *dross* to consume and your gold to refine" (stanza 3).

3. The words "Oh, Come, Oh, Come, Emmanuel" (*LW* 31).

4. "Lord, Now Let Your Servant Depart in Peace" (Nunc dimittis) (*LW*, p. 173).

5. "Hosanna, Loud Hosanna" (*LW* 106).

Answers:

1. From the story of Moses and the Amalekites (Exodus 17:8–15): When Moses held up his hands, the battle with the Amalekites turned in favor of Israel. When his hands got tired and were moved down, the Amalekites started winning. Aaron and Hur held up Moses's hands and, thus, the children of Israel defeated the enemy. We too can be of support to our leaders and "with our prayers and bounties" do what God would have us do.

2. When refining metal, the "dross" is the waste product that forms on the molten surface. In this hymn we are likened to gold which is being refined by God.

3. Emmanuel means "God with us." In this Advent hymn we are praying for God to come and be with us, to ransom us "captives who are in exile." In this hymn we remember the captives in Babylon who waited for the Lord's (Emmanuel's) coming.

4. The words of this song, from Luke 2:29–32, are also known as the Song of Simeon. When Jesus was presented in the temple (Luke 2:21 ff.), it was Simeon who sang this song of praise and thanks to God for having sent his Son to save all the people of the world.

5. Hosanna means "save us." This song relates the story of the triumphal entry of Jesus into Jerusalem (John 12:13). "Hosanna" ("save us") became an expression of praise and joy. When we sing "hosanna," we are praying that God *will* save us and expressing our joy because he *has* saved us—all at the same time.

This kind of basic vocabulary is something too often ignored. We need to take the time to explain the vocabulary and ideas found in hymn texts and then reflect on the meaning of the stanzas.

Familiarize Students with the Basic Liturgies

One of the easiest ways to encourage your children's vigorous partici-

pation in worship is to teach them the liturgy. They can learn it little by little, but learn it they must. Young children can learn to sing the Hymn of Praise, the Alleluia Verse, Gospel responses, the Sanctus ("Holy, Holy, Holy Lord"), the Agnus Dei ("Lamb of God") and the Post-Communion Canticle. Every child should, of course, memorize the Lord's Prayer and the Apostles' Creed.

When we teach parts of the liturgy to our children, we should tell them about where the words come from—just as we do for hymn texts. For example, before the Gospel is read, we sing, "Alleluia. Lord to whom shall we go? You have the words of eternal life. Alleluia, alleluia." These are the words of Simon Peter (John 6:68) as he responds to Christ's question, "You do not want to leave too, do you?" (John 6:67). Peter responds by saying that there in no one else to whom the disciples can turn; only Jesus has the words of eternal life. When other disciples had deserted Jesus, the Twelve remained to listen and learn that Jesus was "the holy one of God." As we explain the scriptural basis for the words that we sing and say, we help children to understand the meaning behind the words. In this way, we help them appreciate the depth of the liturgical forms which they hear on Sunday morning.[2]

Find Out about the Men and Women Who Wrote the Music and the Texts of Hymns

Reading about the lives of those who have composed the tunes and written or translated the hymn texts can be very enjoyable and enlightening. The stories of these musicians, poets, and translators inspire us and can give us new insight into the meaning of the hymns that we love to sing. If you are not sure who wrote a particular hymn, consult your hymnal. The composer of the text and tune of each hymn is usually printed somewhere (probably in small print) on the page where you find the hymn. Authors and composers of the hymns are usually listed in the index section of the hymnbook.

The following hymn writers/composers are interesting to study. These brief statements may give you an idea how you might begin to use the lives of hymnists as examples of personal faith and devotion to Christ.

John Newton (1725–1807)

Familiar hymn texts: "On What Has Now Been Sown," "How Sweet the Name of Jesus Sounds," "Glorious Things of You are Spoken," and "Amazing Grace! How Sweet the Sound" (probably one of the most popular hymns ever written). Newton was a slave dealer who was converted to Christianity. His life is summarized in his epitaph. Newton wrote, "John Newton, Clerk, Once an infidel and libertine, A servant of slaves in Africa, Was, by the rich mercy of our Lord And Savior Jesus Christ, Preserved, restored, pardoned, And appointed to preach the Faith He had long labored to destroy. Near sixty years at Olney in Bucks, And twenty-eight years in this church."

Paul Gerhardt (1606–76)

One of the greatest hymn writers. Four of his five children died in infancy. He lost his position as pastor for refusing to sign an edict that

would limit free speech regarding certain religious questions. He wrote such hymns as: "O Sacred Head Now Wounded," "O Lord, How Shall I Meet You," "A Lamb Goes Uncomplaining Forth," and "Now Rest Beneath Night's Shadow."

Catherine Winkworth (1829–78)

Translated 20 of Paul Gerhardt's hymns from German to English. She, along with a number of English women (such as Francis Cox and Sarah Findlater), translated many hymns. Winkworth is considered the greatest of the English translators of German hymns. Some of her translations include: "All Glory Be to God on High," "Praise to the Lord, the Almighty," "Comfort, Comfort Ye My People," "O Morning Star, How Fair and Bright," and "Jesus, Priceless Treasure."

Charles Wesley (1707–88)

Wesley was a Methodist clergyman who wrote over 6500 hymns including: "Hark, The Herald Angels Sing," "Jesus Christ Is Risen Today," "Oh, for a Thousand Tongues to Sing," and "Love Divine, All Love Excelling."

Isaac Watts (1674–1748)

Watts wrote 600 hymns and 60 books. He was small of stature (five feet) and had a most engaging personality. He went for a one-week visit to the home of Sir Thomas Abney and stayed for 36 years. He was a preacher, writer, and scholar who gave us many hymn treasures including: "Joy to the World," "Alas! and Did My Savior Bleed," and "From All That Dwell Below the Skies." He wrote most of his hymns before he reached the age of 30.

Bellema Kwillia (born circa 1925)

Kwillia wrote the communion hymn, "Come, Let Us Eat." He was born in Liberia and was taught how to read through a literacy program sponsored by the church. While working as a teacher, he became a Christian and later an evangelist to his own town. The translator of the hymn, Margaret D. Miller, notes that it was while Kwillia was a literacy teacher-evangelist that he sang this hymn for a meeting and it was recorded on tape.[3] This is an example of how God works in mysterious and wonderful ways. Here God has used a literacy program, a Christian teacher/evangelist from Liberia, a translator, and a tape recorder to edify Christians throughout the world.

Other favorite hymn writers and composers

Koh Yuki, Seige Abe, St. Francis of Assisi, Jaroslav Vajda, Jan Bender, Johann Crüger, Richard Hillert, Carl Schalk, Phillip Nicolai, Martin Luther, Martin Franzmann.

Take time to tell your students about the lives of the women and men who have given, and who continue to give us, music and words that praise God. Here are some resources that you can use to find out something about the "people behind the hymns."

Hymnal Companion to the Lutheran Book of Worship. Marilyn Kay Stulken. Philadelphia: Fortress Press. © 1981.

The Story of Our Hymns. Armin Haeussler. St. Louis: Eden Publishing House. © 1952.

American Hymns Old and New: Notes on the Hymns and Biographies of the Authors and Composers. Charles W. Hughes. New York: Columbia University Press. © 1980.

The Handbook to the Lutheran Hymnal. W. G. Polack. St. Louis: Concordia Publishing House ©1942.

Lutheran Worship Hymnal Companion. Fred L. Precht. St. Louis: Concordia Publishing House. © 1992.

Activities to Do with Children on "The People Behind the Hymns"

1. Have children make a list of their favorite hymns and then ask them to look up the composer of the hymn text and tune and report on their findings.

2. Have children take on the role of a hymn composer and do a "mini-drama" about that person's life. This could be a "This Is Your Life" kind of presentation.

3. Write to composers and ask them why they write hymns and where they get their ideas for the words and music they compose.

4. Have a hymn sing dedicated to a particular hymn writer.

5. Take a poll of the congregation to find out the "most loved hymns of our congregation." Sing one of the "top ten" hymns during the Bible class/Sunday school hour each Sunday. A brief report on the life of the composers can be given by the youth Bible class members before the singing of the hymn.

6. Ask a composer to visit your class.

Other Activities to Foster Hymn Appreciation

1. Have children write new lyrics to their favorite hymn melodies.

2. Use a hymn as a prayer. Read the stanzas to one another in a dramatic way.

3. Mix and match hymns with the same meters with different tunes. (Using the index of metrical listing for hymns, you can sing hymns with the same meter to different tunes. Every once in a while the hymn text and tune will not "sound right" for each other. Don't let that worry you. This activity is interesting because it helps us to "hear" old hymns in a new way. Try, for example, singing the common meter song "The Lord's My Shepherd, I'll Not Want" to the tune of "Amazing Grace! How Sweet the Sound." This hymn. by the way, can be sung in canon (a round). If you sing "The Lord's My Shepherd" to the "Amazing Grace" tune, you can sing those stanzas in canon as well.[4]

Write New Words to Existing Tunes

Your students work won't rank among the top 10 new hymns of the decade, but it will help the children learn the structure of hymns and the way they present biblical truths.

Here, for example, are some lyrics that can be sung to the tunes of "As with Gladness Men of Old" (Tune: *Dix, LW* 75, *LBW* 82, *TLH* 127), or "Go to Dark Gethsemane" (Tune: *Gethsemane, LW* 110, *LBW* 109, *TLH* 159), or even "Twinkle, Twinkle, Little Star."

1. Advent-Christmas Season

Jesus, Jesus, came to earth
In a stable was his birth
To fulfill what was foretold
In the prophecies of old
Jesus, Jesus, God's own Son
Came to earth to make us one

2. Christmas-Epiphany Season

Wise Men, Wise Men, from afar
Searched by camel for the star
When they found the baby dear
Mary, Joseph, kneeling near
Worshiped him with gifts and praise
Loved and served him all their days

3. Passion Week—The Garden of Gethsemane

Sorrow, sorrow, can this be?
Jesus prayed in agony
Peter, James, and John were there
Fast asleep without a care
Sorrow, sorrow we're in Lent
See how his last hours were spent

4. Passion Week—Before Pilate

(Try stanzas 4–6 to the tune of "Go to Dark Gethsemane")

Jesus, Jesus, all alone
Standing there at Pilate's throne
Whipped and beaten, held to scorn
On his head a crown of thorn
Jesus, Jesus, all alone
Standing there at Pilate's throne

5. Good Friday

Jesus, Jesus, on the cross
He went there to save the lost
And the lost were you and me
Thus he died to set us free
Jesus, Jesus, on the cross
He went there to save the lost

6. Easter

Jesus, Jesus, from the grave
Risen now for us today
He is here with us to stay
Nevermore to go away
Jesus, Jesus, from the grave
Risen now for us today

7. Ascension

Jesus, Jesus, up on high
Then they saw him in the sky
Rising, rising, to the Lord
Into highest heaven soared
Jesus, Jesus, up on high
There they saw him in the sky

8. Pentecost with Doxology

Spirit, Spirit, all on fire
Now disciples are inspired
Fire and wind showed them the way
How to preach and how to pray
Spirit, Spirit, make us one
Praising Father, Spirit, Son

Seven Steps to Writing a New Song to the Tune of a Nursery Rhyme Song

1. First, get your hymnal and keep it handy; you'll use the hymnal later.

2. Count the number of syllables per line of the tune for which you want to write new words. Let's use "Twinkle, Twinkle" as an example.

       1 2   3   4   5 6 7
Line 1. Twin-kle, twin-kle, lit-tle star

       1 2 3   4   5   6 7
Line 2. How I won-der what you are

       1 2 3   4   5 6 7
Line 3. Up a-bove the world so high

       1 2   3   4 5 6 7
Line 4. Like a dia-mond in the sky

       1 2   3   4 5 6 7
Line 5. Twin-kle, twin-kle, lit-tle star

       1 2   3   4   5 6 7
Line 6. How I won-der what you are

3. Next, count the number of lines in the poem. "Twinkle, Twinkle" has six lines, each containing seven syllables. The meter is notated as *77 77 77*. If you look in the back of *Lutheran Worship* (pp. 994–99), you will find a metrical index of hymn tunes. On page 997 of *LW* you will note a number of hymn tunes which are listed under the *77 77 77* meter. The tune *Dix* ("As With Gladness Men of Old," *LW* 75) has the same meter as "Twinkle, Twinkle." Try singing "Twinkle, Twinkle" to the tune of "As with Gladness Men of Old" and vice versa. See how that works. Now try stanzas 3–6 of the example song (Passion Week to Easter) to the tune *Gethsemane* ("Go to Dark Gethsemane," *LW* 110).

When you're finished, you'll be able to use different tunes to your new lyrics. This will enable you to add variety and give new meaning to your words as well.

4. Now let's start with the "formula" beginning—"Jesus, Jesus" (4 syllables) and add words to fill out the remaining **three syllables** in the first line.

1 2 3 4 5 6 7

Line 1. Je-sus, Je-sus, **came to earth**

We could have had all sorts of three syllable endings: came to earth, came from heav'n, from on high, God's own Son, babe so small, etc. Each of these lines would lead to a different rhyme scheme and a very different final lyric.

5. Think of a seven syllable line that ends with a word that rhymes with *earth*. Quickly think of a few words that rhyme with *earth*. Fill in the blanks with as many as you can think of in 15 seconds.

Go!

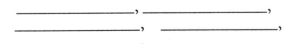

You probably thought of some of these: birth, dearth, girth, mirth, worth. There are, of course, many more. You could use a rhyming dictionary to find more possibili-

ties, but for now let's work with what we've got thus far and add **stressed** and unstressed syllables to complete the second seven-syllable line.

1 2 3 4 5 6 7

Line 1. **Je**-sus, **Je**-sus, **came** to **earth**

Line 2. **In** a **sta**-ble **was** his **birth**

You can feel the stress accents as you speak the words. The accents for this particular song fall as follows: TUM-ta TUM-ta TUM-ta TUM. (TUM-ta is a trochee, for you poetry buffs.)

6. Next, write another rhyming couplet (two lines with a rhyming word at the end of each line). Think of what was happening at the time of Jesus' birth to give a clue as to what the content of the next lines might be. Fulfilling prophecies is what came to mind to the group who wrote the lyrics in the example song. They wrote:

Line 3. **To** ful - **fill** what **was** fore-**told**

Line 4. **In** the **proph**- e- **cies** of **old**

But, they might have written something that described the people at the manger. For example:

Mar- y, **Jo**- seph **and** the **child**
Sleep-ing **soft**-ly **un**- de- **filed**

or

Shep-herds **kneel**-ing **in** the **straw**
An- gels **sing** -ing "**Glo**-ri-a"

Either of these alternate examples could be used. Try several alternate stanzas to discover which lines best tell the story that **you** are trying to tell.

7. You need a final couplet to end the song. This can be done in two ways. The simplest way is to repeat the first two lines of the stanza, as was done in the lyric to "Twinkle, Twinkle," and in stanzas 4, 5, 6, and 7 of the example song. You may wish to write a final couplet that continues the story line of the lyric as was done in the first stanza of the example song:

Line 5. **Je** -sus, **Je** -sus, **God's** own **Son**

Line 6. **Came** to **earth** to **make** us **one**

Try It—You'll Like It

Now it's time for you to try one on your own. Try writing a song based on a parable or an Old Testament story. To add variety, try writing lyrics using other nursery rhyme songs such as "Down by the Station" (56 65 66 7), "Row, Row, Row Your Boat" (55 66 5), or "The Farmer in the Dell" (6666). Get a group of students, teachers, or parents together for a song-writing night. Encourage individual students and teachers to write a stanza of a song. Use your songs in Sunday school, vacation Bible school, Christian day school, at morning classroom devotions, or for an introduction to the reading of the Epistle or Gospel. Print the songs in a booklet and sing them at a hymn festival in church or Sunday school. Post the new lyrics on a bulletin board in your classrooms. Have older children go caroling in the classrooms of younger children and sing a new song for the little ones. Check out the piggyback songs on pp. 107–9 in *Little Ones Sing Praise: Christian Songs for Young Children* (CPH © 1989) for more examples of gospel lyrics set to nursery rhyme songs.

Endless Possibilities ...

The possibilities for writing hymns to nursery rhyme tunes are endless, however, and you need not limit yourself to nursery rhymes tunes. The rhymes and rhythms of nursery songs are useful as starting models for writing because they are familiar to both children and adults. Once you have done a few piggyback songs, try writing new texts to familiar tunes from your hymnal. (Don't forget to use the metrical index in the back of the hymnal: *LW* pp. 994ff.; *LBW* pp. 949ff.; *TLH* pp. 842ff.)

Always remember that you are trying to proclaim the Good News in your texts. Keep the proclamation of the Law and the Gospel at the center of your lyrics so that the story of salvation is understood by both singers and hearers of the song.

There are many ways of using music to tell the story of God's love, forgiveness, mercy, and salvation. Telling the story with new words to old songs is a great way to proclaim the message of God's saving grace.

Family Devotions around the Hymnal

The hymnal is an excellent resource for family devotions. Because the hymnal contains so many resources (e.g., prayers, evening and morning prayer services, psalms, canticles and chants, the Hymn of the Day, etc.), family members can grow in their faith as they use these resources as a basis for daily devotions. When devotions are planned in conjunction with the Sunday morning Scripture readings, children can be helped to understand more of what's happening during the church service. The Scripture lessons which change from Sunday to Sunday are called the "Propers of the Day." The Propers are the readings which are "proper" for that particular Sunday and include the Introit, Scripture readings, Collect, Gradual, Verse, hymns, and prayers.[5] The Propers take you through the entire church year and help to insure that you will hear the entire story of salvation from beginning to end. If your church doesn't use a series of Scripture lessons, ask you pastor to provide you with a list of Scripture lessons that he will be using for his sermons.

Here are some suggestions for using the Propers as a guide for devotions.

1. Ask your pastor for the series of scripture readings that will be used during the current church year. In *Lutheran Worship*, the Propers begin on page 10.[6] Each year a different series of Scripture readings may be used, so you will need to find out the particular series which your pastor will be using.

2. Once you know which series of lessons will be used in your church, use the Propers for the coming Sunday as a basis for your devotions during the week.

Here's an example of how you might use the Propers in devotions:

For the week before the First Sunday in Advent, read the Introit, Collect, and readings that will be read on the First Sunday in Advent. (We will use the one-year series readings for this example).

On Monday: Read or sing the Introit (based on Zechariah 9:9b and Psalm 25). Look for the Hymn of the Day Index (*LW* pp. 976ff.) and sing "Savior of the Nations Come." You will note that this hymn is the Hymn of the Day appointed for the First Sunday in Advent (Advent 1). Read Psalm 50:1–15. After the reading, someone may wish to comment on some of the ideas in the reading like this:

> In the Psalm 50 reading, I was particularly struck by two verses: "Our God comes and will not be silent" (v. 3) and "call upon me in the day of trouble; I will deliver you and you will honor me" (v. 15). Indeed, our God is not silent. God speaks with great power when he sends his Son, Jesus, to be our Savior. At the birth of Jesus the heavens were shaken with the sounds of angels announcing his birth with loud Glorias. We know that God is not silent. He doesn't stand by while we are in trouble and say nothing. He speaks to us through his Son and promises to deliver us. We can be confident that when we call on God he will help us live through the problems that we face. Jesus has come to be the sacrifice for our sins. In this Advent season we are reminded of God's power and compassion. That's way we can pray and sing "Savior of the Nations Come" with confidence. We know that God has come and that he continues to care for us every day.

After comments from our family members, you could pray the Collect of the Day for the First Sunday in Advent (*LW*, p. 10).

On Tuesday: Read Isaiah 2:1–5 and discuss its meaning. A Bible commentary or a study Bible, will help you focus on the meaning of the passage. In this passage, a glance at the notes on the bottom of page 1022 of the *Concordia Self-Study Bible* will help you to understand what this passage refers to. All the nations of the earth are invited to come to "the mountain of the Lord" because of the message which the Messiah will preach. We can "walk in the light of the Lord" because Christ is the light of the world. A "round the table" prayer could be spoken by all the family members and another Advent hymn could be sung or spoken. In keeping with the "light of the world" theme, you could use "O Lord of Light, Who Made the Stars" (*LW* 17) or "The King Shall Come (*LW* 26). Since both of these hymn texts refer to light, they would be appropriate to use as hymns or prayers.

On Wednesday: Before the family goes to evening Advent services, take time to read through the Advent hymns which are part of the evening service. (Ask your pastor or parish organist to make a list of upcoming hymns available to the congregation so you can help your children rehearse the hymns ahead of time). Comment on the meaning of the hymns. When you sing the hymns during the service, you can concentrate better because you have done a preview of the hymns in your family devotion.

On Thursday: Read Romans 13:11–14. Notice the theme of darkness and light again in this passage. This passage urges us to "put aside the deeds of darkness and put on the armor of light" (v. 12) and "wake up from (our) slumber" because "our salvation is nearer now than when we first believed" (v. 11). Comment on the idea that our salvation is near. In Advent we contemplate the coming of our Lord. Jesus has come and will come again. As we prepare ourselves for his coming, we do so by repenting of our sins and holding firmly to his promise of salvation. We are clothed in light. In our Baptism we are made God's own. We are his new creation. We wait for his coming. An appropriate hymn to sing might be "Hark! A Thrilling Voice Is Sounding" (*LW* 18). The text reads, "Hark! A thrilling voice is sounding! 'Christ is near,' we hear it say. 'Cast away the works of darkness, all you children of the day!'" The hymn echoes the words of Romans 13. Finish with one of the prayers found in the "Petitions, Intercessions, and Thanksgivings" section of the hymnal (*LW*, pp. 124 ff.) Use the prayer "For Newness of Life in Christ" (*LW*, p. 125): "Almighty God, give us grace that we may cast away the works of darkness and put upon ourselves the armor of light. ... "

On Friday: Read Matthew 24:37–44 or Matthew 21:1–11. The first Gospel reading urges us to prepared for the coming of the Lord. Advent is about preparation. We prepare for his coming by examining our lives and repenting of our sins. Advent is a time of penitential preparation. We are now ready to meet our Lord and can rejoice because he has come to be our Savior. In the second Gospel reading we sing "Hosanna to the Son of David." Hosanna means "save us." The "save us" is not only a request but a shout of triumph, because we know that God has saved us in his Son, Jesus Christ. Therefore we can shout for joy in the words of the Gradual (*LW*, p. 11): "Rejoice greatly, O daughter of Zion! Shout, daughter of Jerusalem! See, your King comes to you, righteous and having salvation. Blessed is he who comes in the name of the Lord. From the house of the Lord we bless you." God has blessed us and will continue to bless us both now and when we meet him in heaven. Sing or read the hymn "The Advent of Our God" (*LW* 12) as your closing prayer. Think through the hymn in relation to the Scripture readings and the Gradual.

On Saturday: Take a look at the Verse for the First Sunday in Advent (*LW*, p. 11). Note that it is taken from Psalm 24. Read Psalm 24 (*LW*, p. 321,) and stop at the end of each verse to reflect on the meaning of each verse. You may wish to use a commentary or the notes in your Bible to clarify the meaning of the psalm. Follow your discussion with the singing of "Lift Up Your Heads, You Mighty Gates" (*LW* 23 or 24). In both Psalm 24 and the hymn, the gates of the city fling open. God is so great that the top of the gates as well as the doors must burst open at his arrival. Now we pray that God would also open our hearts so that Christ may abide in us. As the last verse of "Lift Up Your Head" states: "Christ Jesus, Lord and Savior, come, I open wide my heart, your home. Oh enter with your radiant grace, on my life's pattern shine your face, and let your Holy Spirit guide to gracious vistas rich and

wide. Our God, we praise your name, forevermore the same. AMEN!"

On Sunday: Look at the readings for the Second Sunday in Advent, and begin the process of preparation for the next week.

On Special Festival Days: Pages 94 ff. of *Lutheran Worship* contain a number of "minor festivals" you and your family can celebrate. Readings and Collects for the days are provided. A family devotional celebration around these minor festivals will be helping to teach your children about the lives of the saints. A good hymn to use when you celebrate a saint's day is "By All Your Saints in Warfare" (*LW* 193). Each stanza is dedicated to a different saint and gives a mini biography. One good resource that you might use for devotions about the saints is Philip H. Pfatteicher's *Festivals and Commemorations* (Augsburg, © 1980). Many children are named after people in the Bible. It is always good for children to know something about the life of the saint after whom they were named. When we read about the lives of the saints, we are given examples of how we, too, might live lives of faith.

The Topical Index of Hymns as a Resource for Devotional Life.

Most hymnals have a topical index. A topical index lists hymns by topics—for example, Assurance, Burial, Celebration, Comfort and Rest, Eternal Life, Healing, Hope, Sickness, and Trust. When you need a hymn to fit a particular occasion, the topical index is a good place to start. The topical index helps you to narrow the field quickly and is a good aid for planning devotions. As you plan your devotions, remember that hymns make excellent prayers.

Use The Morning and Evening Prayer Services Found in *Lutheran Worship* or *Lutheran Book of Worship*

The services of Morning Prayer (*LW*, p. 236; *LBW*, p. 131) and Evening Prayer (*LW*, p. 250; *LBW*, p. 142) are good sources for family devotions. They can be read or sung and have been designed in an abbreviated form for use in the family devotional setting. (The abbreviated form of the service is noted by a small red circle.) You can add your own readings, prayers, hymns, and other devotional material as you see fit within the context of the service. Note that in Evening Prayer the children will read or sing "The Magnificat" ("My soul proclaims the greatness of the Lord"). This song of Mary has been sung by Christians throughout the centuries. When we teach children these classics, we unite them with Christians all over the world. We remind them that Jesus is the fulfillment of the promise which God made to Abraham.

Our hymnals helps us remember the promises of God. Through their songs, liturgies, and prayers we are able to sing "new songs to the Lord" in hundreds of ways. Hymnals are a great gift to the church which need constant exploration. As we help children become more familiar with the hymnal we are giving them a resource which will strengthen their devotional life for the rest of their lives. Like the scriptures, hymnals need to be used every day. Hymns are a continual source of joy and comfort. They remind us of all the wonderful things that God has done for us in his Son, Jesus. When we help children to fully use the hymnal, we are giving them a gift that will truly last a lifetime.

A Final Word

What Makes for a Good Teacher or for Good Teaching?

When people ask me what makes a good teacher, I reply in several ways. One is an academic response regarding the professional characteristics and dispositions of a good teacher. I can try to describe or define what makes for good teaching or a good teacher, but in the final analysis, they defy description. You can't always describe good teaching, but you usually know what it is when you see it.

Sometimes a discussion of the teacher's academic expertise is involved. Discipline, classroom management skills, and preparation are, of course, important. But as important and necessary as these skills and knowledge are, the most important characteristic that a teacher of the faith must possess is *faith*. God calls us to be faithful to him. The most effective ingredient for teaching the faith is the faithful, faith-filled teacher. What makes for a good teacher of the faith? It may defy definition but it takes faith to do it.

When Are You Prepared to Teach the Faith?

Are we ever prepared enough to teach the faith? No and yes. No, because we can never be prepared enough; and yes, because God promises to use us just as we are to accomplish his good purposes. We must remember that when God uses us just as we are, he is using what he has redeemed. That's pretty powerful!

It is important to be as competent as we can be and to be good caretakers of the talents, gifts, and abilities given to us by God. But we also know that we won't always have the correct answers to every question, and we won't always feel that we have done or said the right things. This is where the work of the Spirit is most evident. The Spirit's fire will refine your work and your words, your songs and your service, your prayers and your preparation, into the gold for his service.

The Christlike Life

Someone suggested that the best way to choose teachers of the faith is to select the people of the congregation who lead the most faith-filled lives—and *demand* they teach the faith. Lesson preparation, discipline, management, and other teaching strategies can be learned, but they can't substitute for a personal example of the Christian life which shows children what it means to be a forgiven son or daughter of God.

I pray that you, baptized and redeemed by the blood of Jesus, will live lives of faithful service to the Lord as you instruct God's children in the faith. Children can learn about the "facts and figures" of the faith from Bible reading, worship experiences, and text books, but they will learn more about what living the faith means from you and the Christlike example you exhibit. You may be the only way that some children will ever "see" Jesus. This is the awesome responsibility and privilege that we have as we strive to be faithful servants of God. We will be blessed by God as we go about our teaching tasks in faith. That's God's promise. Whenever we gather in his name, he is with us to strengthen and encourage us.

The next time you prepare your lessons, write a devotion, or practice a puppet play for Sunday school, remember that what you are doing will dramatically affect the faith lives of your children. You will effect them because of who you are: a redeemed and faith-filled child of God. Be confident that God will help you in all you say and do. God will use your faithfulness to expand his kingdom as he works faith in you through his Spirit.

Let's Pray Once More

Gracious God, you have given us the privilege to serve you as we teach your children about your great acts. Help us to be faithful as we go about our teaching tasks. Help us to live Christlike lives so that those we teach may see you in us. Send us your Spirit so that we may ever grow in faith, and be with us as we teach and pray; as we sing and worship, and as we learn to live out our lives in devoted service to you. Thank you for the opportunities and the challenges that you put before us; but most of all, thank you for sending your Son, Jesus, to be our Savior. In his name we pray. Amen.

Now, go and teach with joy in the name of God the Father, who created the world and sustains it; in the name of God the Son, who redeemed us all; and in the name of God the Holy Spirit, who protects, comforts, and keeps us in faith! Amen and AMEN AGAIN!

Appendix A: Resource List

Bibles

People often ask which version of the Bible they should get for personal study and teaching. My response: "As many as you can." When I do personal study of Scripture, I find it helpful to read the same passage in at least two versions. Sometimes I compare four or five versions of the same text to get a better understanding of what Scripture is saying.

When I was a child, I studied from and memorized passages from the King James Version. In high school and college I studied the Revised Standard Version. Today, my version of choice is the *Concordia Self-Study Bible* (St. Louis: CPH, 1986). Of all the Bibles on the market today, this one provides the most tools for study: the NIV text; a color atlas; frequent maps interspersed in the text; a 35,000-word concordance; charts; graphs; timelines; a cross referencing system; introductions, outlines, and background information on each book of the Bible; and, most important of all, exhaustive study notes.

Concordances

Concordances help you find words, phrases, and proper names in the Bible. Along with using a concordance in your own preparation, show your students how you use it. Learning about Bible reference tools is an important part of Christian education. Some suggestions:

Goodrick, E. W., and J. R. Kohlenberger III, eds. *The NIV Exhaustive Concordance to the Bible*. Grand Rapids: Zondervan, 1981.

Strong, James. *Strong's Exhaustive Concordance of the Bible*. Various publishers.

Young, Robert. *Young's Analytical Concordance to the Bible*. New York: Funk & Wagnalls, 1936.

Bible Dictionaries

One-Volume Dictionaries

Achtemeier, Paul J., ed. *Harper's Bible Dictionary*. San Francisco: Harper & Row, 1985.

Douglas, James D., and Norman Hillyer, eds. *The New Bible Dictionary*. Grand Rapids: Eerdmans, 1982.

Douglas, James D., and Merrill C. Tenney. *NIV Compact Dictionary of the Bible*. Grand Rapids: Zondervan, 1989.

Harrison, R. K., ed. *The New Unger's Bible Dictionary*, Revised Edition. Chicago: Moody Press, 1988.

Lueker, Erwin. *Concordia Bible Dictionary*. St. Louis: CPH, 1963.

Multi-Volume Dictionaries

Bromiley, Geoffrey W. *The International Standard Bible Dictionary*. Grand Rapids: Eerdmans, 1988.

Buttrick, George A., ed. *The Interpreter's Dictionary of the Bible*. Nashville: Abingdon, 1962. Supplement, 1976.

Douglas, James D., and Norman Hillyer. *The Illustrated Bible Dictionary* (Revised).

Wheaton: Tyndale, 1980.

Lockyer, Herbert, ed. *Nelson's Illustrated Bible Dictionary*. Nashville: Thomas Nelson, 1986.

Bible Commentaries

One-Volume Commentaries

Laymon, Charles M., ed. *The Interpreter's One-Volume Commentary on the Bible*. Nashville: Abingdon, 1971.

Mays, James L., ed. *Harper's Bible Commentary*. San Francisco: Harper & Row, 1988.

Roehrs, Walter R., and Martin Franzmann. *Concordia Self-Study Commentary*. St. Louis, CPH, 1971.

Multi-Volume Commentaries

Some of these standard Bible commentaries are easily understood, but others are technical and may cause difficulty. Some are not complete, meaning that not every book of the Bible is covered. Use these in conjunction with one-volume commentaries and several translations of the Bible. (By the way, I recommend *The People's Bible Commentary*.)

Buttrick, George A., ed. *Interpreter's Bible*. Nashville: Abingdon, 1951–57.

Henry, Matthew. *Matthew Henry's Commentary on the Whole Bible*. Peabody, MA: Hendrickson, 1985.

Kretzmann, Paul E. *Popular Commentary*. St. Louis: Concordia, 1923.

Lenski, R. C. H. *Interpretation of New Testament Books*. Columbus, OH: Lutheran Book Concern, 1932; Columbus: Wartburg Press, 1943.

Mays, James L., ed. *Harper Bible Commentary*. San Francisco: Harper SF, 1988.

New International Commentary on the Old Testament. Grand Rapids: Eerdmans, 1984.

The People's Bible Commentary. St. Louis, Concordia, 1992– . An excellent resource for Sunday School teachers.

Tyndale New Testament Commentary. Grand Rapids: Eerdmans, 1982.

Tyndale Old Testament Commentary. Downers Grove: InterVarsity, 1991.

Bible Handbooks

Alexander, David, and Pat Alexander, eds. *Eerdman's Handbook to the Bible*. Grand Rapids: Eerdmans, 1987.

Blair, Edward P. *Illustrated Bible Handbook*. Nashville: Abingdon, 1987.

Halley, Henry. *Halley's Bible Handbook*. Grand Rapids: Zondervan, 1927, 1962. Numerous editions.

Bible Atlases

Frank, Harry Thomas. *Atlas of Bible Lands*. Maplewood, N. J.: Hammond, 1977.

Gardner, Joseph L., ed. *Atlas of the Bible: An Illustrated Guide to the Holy Land*. Pleasantville, NY: Reader's Digest, 1985.

May, Herbert, and John Day. *Oxford Bible Atlas*. London: Oxford, 1987.

Pritchard, James B., ed. *The Harper Atlas of the Bible*. New York: Harper & Row, 1987.

Terrien, Samuel. *The Golden Bible Atlas*. New York: Golden Press, 1957.

References for General Information

Everyday Life in Bible Times. Washington, D. C.: National Geographic Society, 1976.

Lueker, Erwin L. *The Lutheran Cyclopedia.* St. Louis: Concordia, 1975.

Metzger, Bruce M., ed. *Great Events of Bible Times.* Garden City, NY: Doubleday, 1987.

Metzger, Bruce M., and Coogan, Michael D., eds. *The Oxford Companion to the Bible.* New York: Oxford University Press, 1993.

Miller, Madeline S., and J. Lane Miller. *Harper's Encyclopedia of Bible Life.* San Francisco: Harper & Row, 1978.

Richardson, Alan. *Theological Word Book of the Bible.* New York: Macmillan, 1050; Macmillan paperback, 1962.

Teringo, J. Robert. *The Land and People Jesus Knew: A Comprehensive Handbook on Life in First-Century Palestine.* Minneapolis: Bethany House, 1985.

Wright, G. Ernest, principal advisor and ed. consultant. *Great People of the Bible and How They Lived.* Pleasantville, NY: Reader's Digest Association, Inc., 1974.

Resources for Children

Picture Books

Here is a brief list of books that relate to children's lives and have an implicit theological message. Some of them simply retell Bible stories. Some of them deal with the breaking of God's laws but do not necessarily give a Gospel answer to the problems presented. That's where you come in. After reading the books, it is important that you provide the children with the Gospel that the book may not have. Evaluate these books yourself to see if you can use them with your classes. Most if not all are available through your local public library. If not, request that the library purchase them. (Note: Some books written for young children are effective also when used with older children and adults.)

Whenever you are at your library, read children's books with an eye for biblical truths they may contain. Call your local Christian bookstore for more suggestions and share your "finds" with your brother and sister teachers of the faith. Make a list of other children's books that you can use in your teaching.

dePaola, Tomie. *Nana Upstairs and Nana Downstairs.* New York: Putnam, 1973.
A story of death and dying, love and maturity.

_____. *Noah and the Ark.* San Francisco: Harper SF, 1985.

_____. *David and Goliath.* Minneapolis: Winston Press, IN, 1983.
These books include cut-out characters that can be used for puppet theater, flannel boards, and overhead silhouette projections.

_____. *Now One Foot, Now the Other.* New York: Putnam, 1992.
Grandfather has a stroke and is nursed back to help by his grandson. This story can relate how we are to care for and love one another as Christ cares for and loves us.

_____. *The Story of the Three Wise Kings.* New York: Putnam, 1983.
In this brilliantly illustrated story of the Wise Men, the forward explains how in Christian tradition the number of kings was established and how they were eventually given names.

_____. *Tomie dePaola's Book of Bible Stories.* New York: Putnam, 1990.
dePaola weaves the NIV biblical text in the retelling of 17 New Testament and 20 Old Testament stories. An index of Bible texts is included.

Kellogg, Steven. *The Island of the Skog.* New York: Penguin (Dial Books for Young Readers), 1973.
Themes of friendship, acceptance of differences, and love are explored in this book about being afraid, lonely, and pretending to be something you're not.

Lavallee, Barbara. *Mama, Do You Love Me?* New York: Scholastic, Inc., 1992.
A story of unconditional love that may be used in connection with Biblical texts about great love (e.g., 1 Corinthians 13).

Lewis, C. S. *The Lion, the Witch, and the Wardrobe.* New York: Macmillan, 1968.
The Chronicles of Narnia, of which this book is a part, presents the story of salvation using the metaphor of Aslan the Lion for Christ. This story is available on audiocassette as well as in video format, produced by the BBC.

Sendak, Maurice. *Pierre.* New York: HarperCollins, 1991.
Pierre doesn't care about anything until a lion eats him up. His parents love him anyway and save the day. All live happily ever after. When you're finished, you might want to discuss the Fourth Commandment ("Honor your father and mother . . .") and 1 Peter 5:7–8, "Cast all your anxiety on him because he cares for you. Be self-controlled and alert. Your enemy the devil prowls around like a roaring lion looking for someone to devour."

Spier, Peter. *Noah's Ark.* New York: Dell, 1992.
_____. *The Story of Jonah.* New York: Doubleday, 1985.
Both of these books relate their Old Testament story through beautiful pictures. The Noah story is a wordless picture book that uses illustrations that are both beautiful and humorous at the same time. The poem in the front part was translated by Spier from *The Flood,* by Jacobus Revius (1586–1658). This poem will make for great reading for young and old alike. It would also make a good action rhyme or echo pantomime. The Jonah story is retold and illustrated in much the same style as *Noah's Ark* and includes four information-packed pages of maps, diagrams, and notes about the story. Spier even includes a detailed diagram of a Phoenician ship of Jonah's time. *Noah's Ark* is also available in a 27-minute videocassette tape (narrated by James Earl Jones) from Lightyear Entertainment.

Viorst, Judith. *Alexander and the Terrible, Horrible, No Good, Very Bad Day.* New York: Macmillan, 1989.
A humorous look at the problems we must face on a day-to-day basis. After you have read the story to children, remind them that God still loves us, in spite of "evidence" to the contrary. Ask the children to relate a time when they had a "terrible, horrible, no good, very bad day." Pray about those times when things don't go right. Remind the children that Jesus went through the most "terrible, horrible, no good, very bad day" for us.

Zolotow, Charlotte. *The Hating Book.* New York: HarperCollins, 1989.
This book deals with the concepts of anger, gossip, misunderstanding of language, parental advice, and forgiveness. When you have finished the book, you may wish to read Ephesians 4:29–32: "Be kind and compassionate to one another, forgiving each other, just as in Christ God forgave you."

Songbooks and a Hymnal for Children and Young Adults

All God's People Sing. (CPH 97-6161).
Lift Up Your Hearts. (CPH 97-5931).
Little Ones Sing Praise: Christian Songs for Young Children. (CPH 97-5868).

Two Musicals

Burkart, Jeffrey E. *Man Overboard.* St. Louis: Concordia, 1995. This musical is based on the book of Jonah.

Folkening, John. *Noah's RemARKable Voyage.* St. Louis: Concordia, 1991. This excellent musical, based on the account of Noah, gets at the heart of the story: God's covenant relationship fulfilled in Jesus' birth, death, and resurrection. A great way to involve all the children of your parish in a witness to the great promises of God. The dialog, written in rhymed verse, is easy for children to memorize. (Leaders Book with piano score and script: CPH 97-6108); Student Book with music and script: CPH 97-6130.)

Puppet Books and Audio-Visual Supplies

Simplicity Puppet Patterns. Found in craft and fabric stores.

Stohs, Anita R. *Praise God With a Paper Plate.* St. Louis: Concordia, 1992.

Sylwester, Roland. *The Puppet and the Word.* St. Louis: Concordia, 1983.

35mm write-on slides and slide mounts can be purchased through Porter's Camera Store, Cedar Falls, Iowa (1-800-221-5329). You can purchase almost any photographic product through Porter's.

"Crayola Multi-Cultural Washable Markers." Available from toy stores, art stores, and book and stationary stores.

"Multi-Cultural Puppets." Available from Constructive Playthings, Grandview, MO (1-800-488-4115).

Transparencies, frames, colored adhesives, lamination, and other A-V products can be ordered through your local A-V supply house. Call your local elementary or high school's media specialist to get the best information on where to purchase A-V materials. If you are in an area that has limited A-V suppliers, call the Highsmith Co. (1-800-558-2110).

Appendix B:
Letter and Number Blackline Master

Make a transparency of these letters and numbers. Project them with an overhead projector and trace them on paper or cardboard. Make several sets of letters for use on your bulletin boards.

ABCDEFGHIJKLM
NOPQRSTUVWXYZ
1234567890 ?"",:+-
#$& abcdefghijklm
nopqrstuvwxyz
ABCDEFGHIJKLM
NOPQRSTUVWXYZ
1234567890 ?"",:+-
#$& abcdefghijklm
nopqrstuvwxyz

ABCDEFGHIJK
LMNOPQRSTUV
WXYZ 123456789
0 ? " ",:+-#$& abcd
efghijklmnopqrst
uvwxyz
ABCDEFGHIJK
LMNOPQRSTU
VWXYZ 1234567
890 ? " ",:+-#$&
abcdefghijklmno
pqrstuvwxyz

ABCDEFGHIJKL
MNOPQRSTUVW
XYZ123456789
0 ? " " , : + - # $ & a b
cdefghijklmnop
qrstuvwxyz
ABCDEFGHIJKLM
NOPQRSTUVWX
YZ1234567890
? " " , : + - # $ & abcd
efghijklmnopqr
stuvwxyz

Appendix C: Grid for Homemade Slides

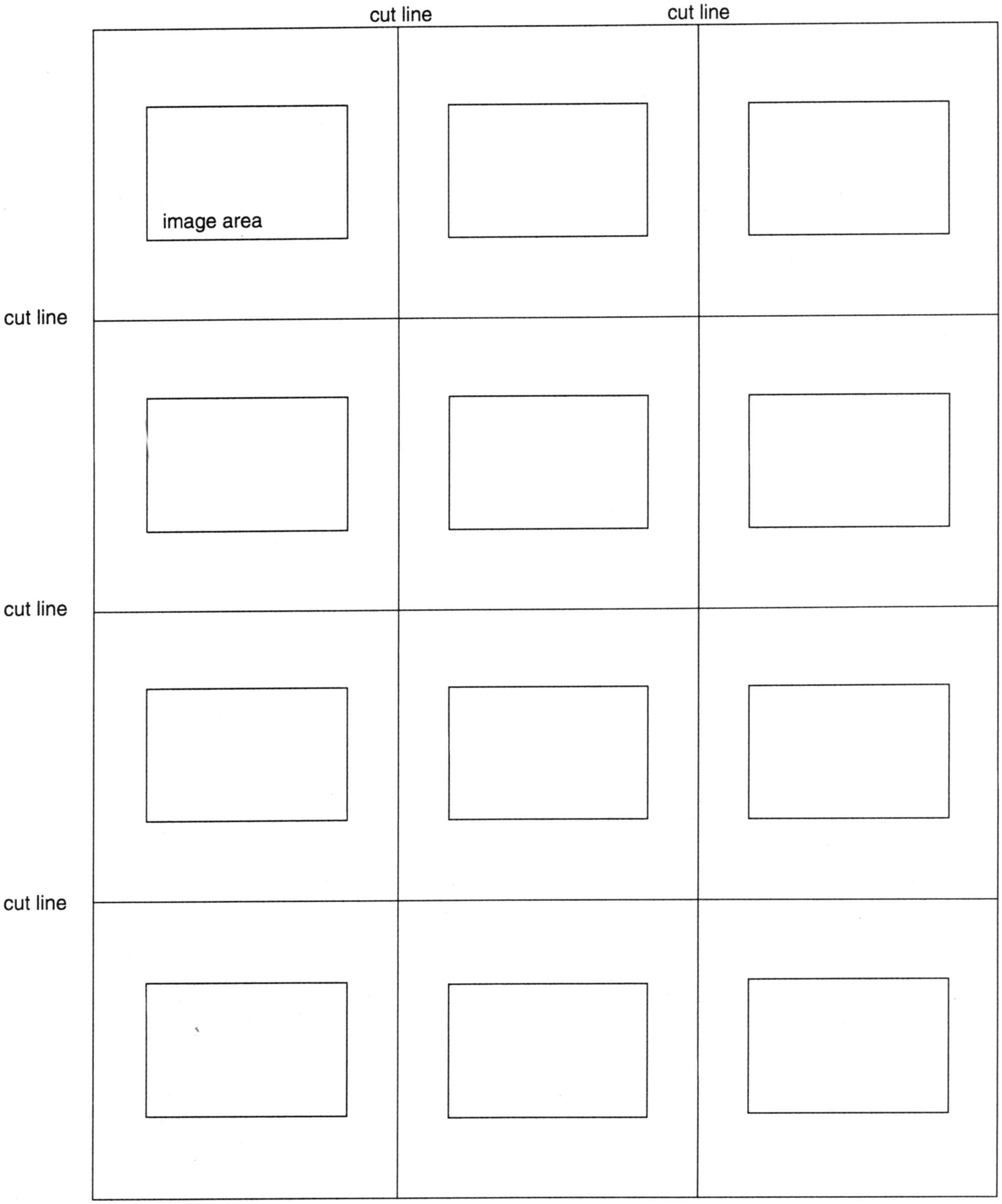

cut line   cut line

cut line

image area

cut line

cut line

Lay acetate sheet over grid. Draw pictures within image area. Cut out acetate
squares and affix inside slide frames. Seal with iron.

Endnotes

Chapter 3

1. Arch Books® are a great resource for teachers. They are stories from the Bible written in poetic form that can be used in a variety of ways. The Concordia Publishing House catalog has a complete listing of these engaging children's Bible story books.

2. Check out Tomie de Paola's *Book of Bible Stories,* or Peter Piper's *Noah and the Ark,* at your public library for starters. See the Resource List for more suggestions.

3. O wad some Pow'r the giftie gie us
   To see oursels as ithers see us! *Robert Burns*
   (Translated it means: Use a mirror or video recorder to see what you look like.)

Chapter 4

1. Here is a little tip. Whenever I find a significant diagram, such as the one I just told you about, I take a marking pens and color just a little of the edge of the page. When the Bible is closed the color stands out on the edge of the book so I can quickly find the diagram I'm looking for. The only problem is that I'm finding so many neat things that the edges of my Bible are getting a little too full of colors. You can also use little paste-on tabs or tape for quick referencing.

Chapter 13

1. I have based this list on the hymnal *Lutheran Worship*. Other hymnals will differ, but these items are generic enough to be found in most hymnals.

2. An excellent short book about worship is *Worship Is* by Walter M. Schoedel and David W. Christian (CPH order no. 22–2387, 1990). This book is an excellent resource for people who want to learn and teach about the order of worship, symbols of the church, the church year, common vocabulary used in worship services, and other aspects of worship that often go unnoticed or are misunderstood.

3. This information was taken from Marilyn Kay Stulken's *Hymnal Companion to the Lutheran Book of Worship* (Fortress Press, 1981), p. 294. The book is an excellent resource for learning about the origins of hymns and the people who write them.

4. The name of the hymn tunes are usually different from the common names of hymns. The name of the tune or melody to "Amazing Grace! How Sweet the Sound" is *New Britain*. When musicians refer to the hymn tune, they are talking about the tune, not the first line of the hymn text.

5. The Propers are distinguished from the parts of the service which make up the Ordinary. The Ordinary parts of the service are those that are done every week and do not change. We "ordinarily" use these parts of the service each week. The Ordinary includes the Invocation, Confession and Absolution, Kyrie, Hymn of Praise, Creed, Preface, Sanctus, Lord's Prayer, Words of Institution, Peace, Agnus Dei, the Post-Communion Canticle and Prayer, and the Benediction.

6. You will find the Prayers of the Day, Psalms, and Lessons starting on page 13 of *Lutheran Book of Worship* and a Daily Lectionary starting on page 179. The Propers can be found beginning on page 54 in *The Lutheran Hymnal.*

Phone Numbers

For quick reference, write the names, addresses, and phone numbers of salespeople, media specialists, librarians, etc., on the lines below:

A-V Supply House and Salesperson

Book Store

Camera Store and Salesperson

Hardware Store

Librarian: Children's Materials

Librarian: Reference

Library

Lumberyard

Media Specialist(s), College/University

Media Specialist, Grade/High School

Newspaper

Paint Store

Stationery Store

Toy Store

_____

_____

_____

TV-Cable: Station Access

_____

_____

_____

Others

_____

_____

_____

_____

_____

_____

_____

_____

Sunday School Teacher Phone Network

List fellow Sunday school teachers as well as other people who have expertise whom you can call to get advise. You might include local Christian school teachers, Directors of Christian Education, pastors, and other church leaders and teachers.

Name _____

Phone _____

Expertise/Address _____

_____

_____

_____

_____

_____

Name _____

Phone _____

Expertise/Address _____

_____

_____

_____

_____

_____

Name _____

Phone _____

Expertise/Address _____

_____
_____
_____
_____
_____
_____

Name _____

Phone _____

Expertise/Address _____

_____
_____
_____
_____
_____
_____

Name _____

Phone _____

Expertise/Address _____

_____
_____
_____
_____
_____
_____

Name _____

Phone _____

Expertise/Address _____

_____
_____
_____
_____
_____
_____